DEMYTHOLOGIZING
AND HISTORY

FRIEDRICH GOGARTEN

DEMYTHOLOGIZING
AND HISTORY

When things move upon bad hinges,
an' please your lordships,
how can it be otherwise?

LAURENCE STERNE
Tristram Shandy

SCM PRESS LTD
56 BLOOMSBURY STREET
LONDON

The present translation by Neville Horton Smith
is based on the first German edition
published in Stuttgart in 1953 under the title
ENTMYTHOLOGISIERUNG UND KIRCHE
by Friedrich Vorwerk Verlag.
For this English version certain changes and
omissions have been made by the author.
First English edition 1955

Printed in Great Britain by
The Camelot Press Ltd., London and Southampton

Contents

I

The Reason for the Controversy

I T is not by chance that the problem of the demythologization, as it is called, of the New Testament is having such wide repercussions. Responsible spokesmen of the Church regard it as a 'terrifying slogan' and a 'deadly dangerous attack upon the foundations and content of belief and of the Church's message'. The general synod of the United Evangelical Lutheran Church of Germany has declared in a unanimous resolution that it 'regards with grave disquiet the danger that God's acts of salvation may in the formulation and propagation of the Church's doctrine be relegated to the background, reduced to mere abstractions and finally abandoned'. It is in fact the case that the questions which this problem raises do not merely concern particular details of the Christian faith or particular conceptions which have traditionally been employed in proclaiming its message. They concern the Christian faith as a whole. For they have to do with the reality in which the Christian faith believes and upon which it is founded, and they call this reality in question, not indeed at all with the intention of denying it but in the conviction that it is necessary to subject to a searching examination the accuracy and pertinence of that traditional interpretation of it by which the Church's teaching is commonly governed. Yet all those who cling to the traditional interpretation as the correct and only possible one are convinced that the carrying through of this

7

theological programme of 'demythologization' would only leave room for 'miserably little' to be said about the divine reality by which faith stands or falls.[1] And Bishop D. Haug, in a speech delivered at the fourth Württemberg Church Congress, has declared that the application of this method to the re-wording and re-interpretation of the New Testament leads to 'positively shattering consequences'. Admittedly, he says, the resulting belief and message do not involve the direct 'denial and elimination of the great acts of God, the facts of salvation as they are called (the Son of God incarnate, crucified, risen and come again; the Christ outside ourselves, of whom, as we understand it, the New Testament is speaking when it proclaims Christ for us, that we may recognize Christ and ourselves anew in Him)', but these things are 'placed beyond the range of existential knowledge and reduced to the bare fact of the crucifixion of the poor man Jesus which the historian can ascertain, reduced, that is to say, practically to the dimensions of a geometrical point. According to this reading the objective foundation upon which every statement of belief contained in the New Testament rests vanishes from the field of vision of man, confined as he is within his own sphere; and the truths to which the New Testament bears witness, the universal history of salvation and the fullness of salvation in Christ, are reduced to a bare minimum. The practical consequence of this interpretation is a message which retains little contact with the basis and contents of the message of our Church.'[2]

[1] 'Statement on Bultmann's theology. A declaration by the Regional Brotherhood Council (*Landesbruderrat*) of the Württemberg Protestant Interdenominational Organization (*Evangelische Bekenntnisgemeinschaft*).' Published in the periodical 'Arbeit und Besinnung' (*Work and Reflection*). 1950, p. 21.

[2] *Evangelisches Gemeindeblatt für Württemberg*, Stuttgart, 18th February, 1951, p. 3.

Despite the negative term 'demythologizing' by which this new kind of 'rewriting and reinterpretation' of the New Testament is designated, it is not in fact true to say that its adherents wish to deny the divine reality of the revelation to which the Bible bears witness and in which Christian faith believes. On the contrary, what they are seeking is in fact identical with what their 'orthodox' opponents believe them to be rejecting, namely the comprehension of this same reality in terms of belief. They are, however, convinced that this 'comprehension in terms of belief' must be achieved in a fundamentally different way from the way which these opponents envisage. They reject the view that the knowledge of this reality 'must precede belief, so that belief may rest upon it just as any other conviction rests upon facts already ascertained.[1] Consequently the purpose of this new theological approach, which has unfortunately acquired the name 'demythologization', is to call for a radical reconsideration of the actual nature and essence of Christian belief.[2] This reconsideration brings with it indeed a fundamentally different understanding of the reality upon which faith is based from that which is accepted by the opponents of the new approach, so that it seems to these opponents that the reality which would remain after such a 'demythologizing' reading of the New Testament would be merely a human reality and not God's reality.

The conflicting points of view in this controversy can only be understood in the light of the causes from which it has arisen. It is widely supposed—and indeed on both sides—that the object of the discussion is to achieve an understanding of Christian belief which is compatible with the thought of our

[1] Bultmann, *Kerygma und Mythos*, II, p. 207.
[2] Bultmann, *Kerygma und Mythos*, II, p. 200.

day, that the controversy arose in the name of modern thought and is being carried on with modern thought in view. It is not indeed suggested that its purpose is to relieve modern thought of the necessity of making a difficult decision, without which there can be no Christian faith, or to make belief 'easy' for it, but rather that it aims at enabling modern thought simply to know once again what Christian faith involves. This opinion is certainly not incorrect, and there is no doubt a need for endeavours of this kind, which, instead of simply declaring modern thought to be entirely false, help it to understand what is meant by belief. But one would be taking a totally inadequate view of the object of the controversy if one were to suppose that its sole purpose was to enable modern thought to assume its rightful place. It is concerned with very much more than that. It is the Christian faith itself which demands its due, and it is for its sake that the controversy must be pursued. It is only in this way that that limited objective too can be achieved.

In order to understand this, two facts must be clearly borne in mind. First, the fact that this controversy is concerned with a radically different interpretation of history. On both sides it is known, or thought to be known, that the reality which underlies the Christian faith is a historical one. But the two sides attach quite different meanings to this historical reality. What the one side understands as historical is for the other side not historical at all. The second fact which must be borne in mind, in order to understand what this controversy is actually about, is that history as a problem, in the sense in which we are here necessarily using the word, arose only with and as a consequence of the Christian faith. The problem of history in this sense arises from the fact that history is no longer seen as a process within a stationary (i.e. supra-historical) world, but, 'on the contrary, the world and man's entire relation to it are themselves involved in history. It is not, as in pre-Christian times, the world, but history itself which constitutes the all-embracing problem.'[1] The problems with which this view of history confronts the Christian faith—they have been the most essential and difficult problems of theology for at least two hundred years and they also have a very direct bearing on 'demythologization'—are not therefore, in whatever form they may arise, problems which impinge upon the faith from without. They spring from the faith itself. The problem of history reflects the original historical nature of the Christian faith and demands an understanding of it. It is only when this understanding is achieved, as it is originally implied in the Christian faith, that there is hope of solving the problems which this faith has encountered in history. We will begin by discussing this second aspect of the matter.

[1] Gerhard Krüger, *Die Geschichte im Denken der Gegenwart* (*History in Present-Day Thought*), p. 14.

II

The Historical View of the Bible

THE problem of history, as it confronts modern theology, first became apparent in the historical view of the Bible, that is to say in the interpretation of the Bible, both as regards its origin and as regards its contents, as a historical book like other historical books. However revolutionary a contrast with the earlier attitude this view may at first have presented, in the course of the past two hundred years it has come to be so generally accepted that no serious theologian can now question it. Its validity is consequently recognized even by the strictly 'official' theology of the Church, which now admits that what the Bible says is said by men and does not derive its authority from the fact that it is written in the Bible. It is rather the Bible which derives its authority simply and solely from what is said in it. No serious theologian nowadays will wish to maintain that one must begin by accepting the truth of the miraculous origin of the Bible, its 'verbal inspiration' as it is called, before one can believe what is written in it. In view of its historical origin he will rather say that reliance upon its testimony can be justified only by belief in what it testifies to. Thus the historical view of the Bible has made it impossible to regard it—to use the terminology favoured by the opponents of 'demythologization'—as the 'objective' basis of belief.

It is important to bear clearly in mind that this does not actually introduce any new factor into the relation between faith and the Bible. On the contrary, the old relationship, as it was before the doctrine of verbal inspiration arose in the period of the old Protestant orthodoxy, has now, certainly in a very remarkable way, been restored. It is of course true that the Bible, as the document of the divine revelation, was for more than a thousand years an unquestioned prerequisite of the Christian faith. But in this respect it was only one of the elements of the metaphysical thinking of the time, that is to say of what might, on the analogy of modern thinking, be called the 'outlook' (*Weltanschauung*) of the early and late middle ages. It was not a prerequisite in the sense that faith as such was based upon it. Faith was based in that period rather upon the Church and her sacramental reality. It was consequently from this sacramental Church, as Roman Catholic theology understands it, and from her authority, that the Bible too derived its religious validity. Luther on the other hand, teaching that the Bible rests solely and entirely upon the Word of God to which it bears witness, drew a very clear distinction between a faith which consists merely in regarding as true the facts vouched for by the Bible, i.e. the *weltanschaulich* faith of the middle ages which he calls the *fides historica*, and the faith which is directed towards the intention of God for man as it is displayed in these facts. The only true faith is that which corresponds to this divine intention. And so, as Luther puts it, it is not the facts themselves, as they are related in the Bible, but it is the 'for me' and the 'for us' seen in them by faith, which, if they are believed, constitute true faith and distinguish it from any other belief which merely holds the historical events, the *res gestae*, to be true.[1] It thus becomes clear that according to Luther it is not upon the book as such or upon its miraculous origin that faith is grounded. The foundation of

[1] Luther, *Werke* (Weimar edition), 39, I, 46.

faith is, on the contrary, the Word by which God promises Himself to mankind as their God. Certainly this Word is vouched for by the Bible, but it is not for that reason that it commands belief, but because it is God's promise, the *promissio dei*. In order to understand this relation between faith and the Word it must of course be realized what a profound and intensely significant meaning Luther attached to the expression 'the Word of God'. I gave some indication of this meaning already when I described the Word upon which faith is founded as the Word by which God promises Himself to mankind as their God. What this is intended to convey is that this Word does not speak *about* the relation of God to man but that the relation itself *arises* with the Word, that is to say by God's speaking it.[1] What this Word means and what happens through God's speaking it Luther repeatedly explained to himself by reference to the first commandment, the saying 'I am the Lord thy God', and in particular the possessive 'thy' which he admits to be in the whole of holy scripture the word which he finds most difficult.[2] 'Thy' is difficult for him because it contains God's promise of Himself and so implies everything which it is the task of faith to believe. In another place he says: 'In it you will find Christ, life, victory over death and the resurrection of the dead to life eternal, indeed the whole of the Old and the New Testament.'[3] This Word is not like a human word, which 'is not of the essence and does not convey the nature of the heart but is a mere representation or sign'. God's Word 'is so much one with God that the whole Godhead is contained within it and whoever has the Word has the whole Godhead'. For in this case 'the Word does not convey merely

[1] Cf. Gogarten, *Der Mensch zwischen Gott und Welt* (*Man between God and World*), pp. 234ff.

[2] Luther, *Tischreden* (Weimar edition), 2, 303.

[3] Luther, *Werke* (Weimar edition), 43, 221.

the sign and the image but also the whole essence and is as full of God as He whose image or Word it is'. 'The Word conveys the whole essence of the divine nature.'[1] The relation between God and man which arises through God's utterance of this Word, in which He promises Himself to mankind with His entire divinity, is characterized precisely by the fact that it arises through and in this Word. This, in turn, means that it arises between God Himself and man himself, or, as we may also put it, between the two as persons. And that, again, means that in hearing this Word, or more precisely in hearing this Word with faith, an event takes place in man which is the meaning of the Word, namely that he lives with the life with which God lives.[2] Thus Luther is able to say of faith in this Word that it is nothing other than the true life in God Himself.[3] If this is the Word upon which faith is founded, it is at once clear that it does not derive its authority from the fact that it is vouched for in the Bible, but that on the contrary the Bible derives its authority from the fact that it testifies to this Word.

It goes without saying that all this is not intended as meaning that the Bible as a book is a matter of indifference. Since the Word upon which faith is based is testified to by the Bible, the Bible derives from it its due authority, which is certainly not inconsiderable. But it is not upon this authority that faith lives, for faith can live upon no other authority than the Word of God itself. Otherwise it would not in any case be possible to say of faith that it is nothing other than the true life in God Himself, or, what amounts to the same thing, that it is a justifying faith. Thus the historical view does indeed

[1] Luther, *Werke* (Weimar edition), 10, I, 1, 188 and 186.
[2] Luther, *Werke* (Weimar edition), 43, 22.
[3] Luther, *Werke* (Weimar edition), 44, 717.

rob the Bible of that which gave it its authority for the *weltanschaulich* thought of the middle ages, namely that metaphysical quality which medieval thought ascribed to it in regarding it as a book of miraculous origin, a quality which lent authority to everything it says, not only in its religious content but also in all its *weltanschaulich* assertions. Since faith, however, is not founded upon this authority of the Bible but solely upon the Word—the promise of God to which the Bible testifies—the historical view of the Bible involves no change in the actual relation of faith to the Bible beyond what is required by the essential nature of this Word and of the faith which accords with it. On the other hand faith is obliged to reflect upon the essential nature of this Word, and upon its own essential nature. But this recognition of the historical nature of the Bible is only the initial and most peripheral application of the historical approach in the field of belief. And since the Bible is not in itself the Word of God upon which faith is founded but only the means by which it is transmitted, and since the authority of the Word of God is not supported by the authority of the Bible, but the Bible derives its authority from the Word of God which is transmitted in it, and since the Word, being the Word of God, carries its authority within itself, it follows that recognition of the historical nature of the Bible implies, in the first instance at least, a new view of the tradition of the Word but not a new view of the Word itself or, therefore, of faith.

But it is in the nature of the historical approach that once it has set to work it does not stop short at the tradition but concerns itself also with that which the tradition conveys. And in the case of the Bible this is not only a word but also, very closely connected with the Word, a series of events. It is that series of events which in theological parlance is called 'the

history of salvation' or 'redemptive history' (*Heilsgeschehen*).
The centre of this 'redemptive history' is the life, the death,
and the resurrection of Jesus Christ. It is only at this point,
where the historical approach sets about its own interpretation
of this 'redemptive history', that it comes to grips with faith.
For it is upon these 'redemptive events' that faith is founded.
Here, then, theology is confronted by the most difficult but
also the most pressing question which exists for it today. This is
the question of the relation between faith and history.

III

The Problem of History an Outcome of Christian Belief

THERE are two reasons why the historical approach, once it has set to work, does not stop short at the tradition, that is to say in our case at the Bible, but concerns itself also with that which the tradition transmits, that is to say the 'redemptive history'. The first reason, more superficial than the other, arises from what is called 'the historical (*historisch*) method'. What this means in its application to historical reality is very clearly shown by the assertion in Ernst Troeltsch's essay, *What is meant by 'the essence of Christianity'?*[1] that ' "purely historical" implies a whole philosophical outlook' (*Weltanschauung*). But, he adds, this is 'not an arbitrary or individual outlook; it is the attitude, based upon innumerable penetrating reflections and verified by innumerable successes, which man assumes towards memories and accounts of the past.'[2] The essential feature of this 'historical method' is that 'by criticism, analogy and correlation, quite of its own accord and by an irresistible necessity, it leads to the construction of an interdependent web of manifestations of the human mind which are at no point isolated and absolute but are everywhere connected and which can likewise be understood only in the context of a whole which so far as possible includes everything'.[3] Since the 'historical method' is governed in this way

[1] *Was heisst 'Wesen des Christentums'?*
[2] Troeltsch, *Gesammelte Schriften*, Vol. II, p. 397.
[3] Troeltsch, *Gesammelte Schriften*, Vol. II, p. 734.

by the idea of a historical whole, Troeltsch is able to say that 'once it is applied to biblical studies and Church history it is a leaven which transforms everything and ultimately explodes the entire existing form of theological methods'.[1] There can be no doubt that in history, as it is understood in the light of this historical method which modern historiography has elaborated, man occupies a different position from that which was previously adjudged him in the general context of the world. It is not an overstatement to say that his position has become so central that this history is now his own, the history of man. And this idea, the idea that it is his own history, means in its deepest sense that he, man, is responsible for history. Thus it is not a question of scientific method alone if the 'historical method' in its investigation of history aims at the 'construction of an interdependent web of manifestations of the human mind' or if, as Dilthey expresses it, it is used 'to seek out the motives of historical movements within humanity itself'.[2] It is rather the expression of the fact that modern man is able to envisage history only from the point of view of his own responsibility for it. This responsibility relates not only to the particular historical decisions of his life, but, at least in intention, to history as a whole, that is to say to history as the history of the world of man. And surely precisely this is the grasping of the actual essential nature of history, or, as we may also express it, of the historical character[3] (*Geschichtlichkeit*) of human existence.

It now becomes possible to see the second reason why the

---

[1] Troeltsch, *Gesammelte Schriften*, Vol. I, p. 730.

[2] Dilthey, *Gesammelte Schriften*, Vol. II, p. 380.

[3] In other translations from the writings of German existential philosophers and theologians the word *Geschichtlichkeit* has been rendered by 'historicity'. In the present work the word 'historicity' is required for *Historizität*, and it then bears its usual English meaning and implies no necessary antithesis to 'metaphysical'. TRANSLATOR.

historical approach, once it has set to work, cannot stop short at the tradition. In order to understand the full significance of this we must go further back. There is indeed a widespread conviction among theologians that the modern historical school's interpretation of history which finds its expression in the 'historical method', precisely because man occupies such a central position in it, is part and parcel of the great apostasy from Christian belief which is supposed to be a general feature of the modern age. Be that as it may, there is nevertheless ground for asking whether this historical approach, at least in so far as it grasps the actual essential nature of history, does not once more bring to the forefront the genuinely Christian view of human existence and of its world as a historical world. For if, without prejudice to whatever else may have to be said about history and the character of history, its essential feature is that man bears the responsibility for it as a whole, that is to say for all the events of the world, it is in the concept of sin, as the Christian faith understands it, that the historical nature of human existence finds its explanation. For since man by his sin, namely by worshipping the creature instead of the Creator,[1] has entirely reversed the true nature of the world and has delivered it up to the bondage and vanity of corruption,[2] it follows that he is answerable for this as surely as he is answerable for his sin. I have said that this genuinely Christian view of human existence and of its world as a historical process has re-emerged in the modern approach to history which is governed by the critical historical method. For in the conception of history which has been superseded by this modern approach, that is to say in the medieval conception of history, the genuinely Christian view of human existence was obscured.

[1] Rom. 1.25.   [2] Rom. 8.19ff.

IV

The Medieval Conception of History

IN the work in which he sets out his principles, the *Introduction to the Sciences of the Mind*,[1] where he describes the supremacy and decline of the metaphysics which for two thousand years dominated the entire philosophical life of the West, Dilthey speaks of this medieval view of history as the 'sublime conception of the middle ages which took its place side by side with the metaphysics of nature, the creation of the Greek mind'. It is, he says, 'quite different from the attitude of the ancients. The ancients had formed their conception of deity in accordance with the cosmos, and even their teleological systems recognized no more than a conformity to thought in the organization of the universe.'[2] In this idea of the world's 'conformity with thought' the ancients, and Dilthey is here thinking especially of the Greeks, were seeking to grasp the world in its unalterable stability. For them the actual reality of the world consisted not in its changing, not, that is to say, in its history, but in its unalterable being. 'All changes in the meaning and ordering of human life were understood in relation to this element of stability. And since it too had its difficulties it presented a far more urgent problem than did history. That is one reason why the historical stream of events itself was not yet seen and understood at all as we now see and

[1] *Einleitung in die Geisteswissenschaften.*
[2] Dilthey, *Gesammelte Schriften*, Vol. I, p. 329f.

21

understand it. It was not yet envisaged as being so profound
and problematic as it is today. The Greeks, who in other fields
discovered almost all our underlying problems, found no
philosophical question of principle at all in this.'[1] In the
medieval historical view, on the other hand, 'God enters into
history and directs men's hearts towards the realization of His
purpose. Consequently the conception of the conformity of
the world to thought is superseded by that of the realization
of a plan in the world, a plan for which the old "conformity to
thought" is only a means or instrument. A goal for the process
of development is established, and thus the idea of purpose
acquires a new significance, namely a historical one.' In this
way the medieval conception of history 'drafted a grandiose
theological scheme of the organization of historical life'.[2]
The outline of this universal history is found in the will and
plan of God as they are proclaimed in the biblical revelation.
'Mankind is a unit, an individual as it were, and as such must
pass through the various stages of a life, but, since he is a pupil,
the rules for this development must mainly come to him from
his Teacher, who educates him according to a plan.' Within
this framework whatever is known about historical processes
from tradition or experience without any investigation of
particular details is 'combined by means of a teleological
interpretation into a coherent whole'.[3]

Just as the contents of a play are established beforehand in
the major and minor rôles which appear in it, so too the events
of this history are given in advance in the 'spiritual substances
of all the orders', which 'are united in the Church as a mystical
body, which extends from the Trinity and the angels which

[1] Gerhard Krüger, *Die Geschichte im Denken der Gegenwart*, p. 8.
[2] Dilthey, *Gesammelte Schriften*, Vol. I, p. 333.
[3] Dilthey, *Gesammelte Schriften*, Vol. I, p. 348.

are nearest to Them down to the beggar at the church door and to the serf who kneels humbly in the obscurest corner of the church to receive the sacrifice of the Mass'.[1] But this interpretation of history as a kingdom of metaphysical essences or substances, motivated teleologically within itself and comprising the whole world within this teleology, allows no historical significance to precisely that which we regard as the actual historical process, namely the vital personal experiences of particular individuals in their particular characters and responsibilities. This loses its historical significance because history anticipates it by taking place within the framework of those metaphysical beings. And it is only in so far as they enter into this metaphysical framework that man's life and its events have a place in the history which unfolds there. Thus, for example, the life and death of the individual medieval man is 'not *his* life and not *his* death; it is not his own but the life and death of all men, which has meaning only if he feels himself to be a member of a community which is united by a common fate. And precisely that which seems to him to be most his own, his deepest experiences, carries his thoughts beyond himself, as a particular historical man, towards that which is common to all mankind. Each suffers the pains of all; each dies the death which has become the lot of all.' Consequently it is not the historical uniqueness of the life of each individual which constitutes the substance of this medieval history, but the metaphysical and general which is established in advance of the historical and particular, and from which the historical and particular alone derives a significance.[2] It is with the twelfth-century movements towards a more spiritual and subjective interpretation of the Christian faith, and

[1] Dilthey, *Gesammelte Schriften*, Vol. I, p. 337.
[2] Bernhard Groethuysen, *Philosophische Anthropologie*, p. 99.

especially with Bernard of Clairvaux and Abélard, that the middle ages begin to come to an end.[1]

Thus although the medieval conception of history attempted for the first time, with a magnificent systematic construction, to interpret the world and man as a historical reality, the genuinely Christian view of human existence and of its world as a historical world was submerged beneath the metaphysics by which this conception was dominated. Why this happened is immediately clear if it is borne in mind that this conception of history was based upon the metaphysical interpretation of the Christian faith, which received its classic form in the christological and trinitarian dogma of the ancient Church through the work of the Church Fathers and the first four general councils, and upon the sacramentalism of the Roman Church which is inseparable from this metaphysical interpretation of the faith.

[1] Cf. Friedrich Heer, *Der Aufgang Europas* (*The Rise of Europe*).

V

Modern Historical Thought

THE significance for Christian belief of modern historical thought and of the 'historical method' which is characteristic of it can be understood only against the background of this medieval conception of history. It must be noted first of all that the application of the 'historical method' has to an increasing extent led to the breaking up of the peculiar combination of historical and metaphysical thinking which is found in the medieval theology of history. But that is not all. The 'historical method' as such is after all only a means for the scientific development and direction of historical thinking in research, and since it is essentially a 'critical' method its relevance and effectiveness must be subject to continual re-examination. What is more important than the 'historical method' is this historical (*geschichtlich*) thinking itself. Troeltsch's remark about the *Weltanschauung*, neither arbitrary nor merely individual, which goes together with the 'historical method' and which represents 'the attitude, confirmed by innumerable penetrating reflections and innumerable successes, which man assumes towards recollections and records of the past' this remark applies not only, and indeed not even primarily, to the historical understanding of the past. This historical approach is rather the expression of a profound change which has taken place since the beginning of the modern age in the relation of man to the world and to himself. This change means nothing

25

more and nothing less than that by it the world has for man become his own world. It is his world now no longer in the sense that it is set before him with its form as a world, its 'being a world' (*Weltsein*), to which it is his task to adapt himself in accordance with its pre-established order. It now becomes his world in the totally different sense that it is for him to watch over it and to provide it with a form and order. And it is in this way as never before that the world becomes for man a truly historical world. And by the same token man himself now becomes the fundamentally historical being who does not merely 'himself creatively render possible his own outlook on life and the world',[1] but also, by his historical decisions in politics, religion, cultural matters, economics, technology and the rest, gives the world the particular form in which it makes possible for a man a life that is in accordance with his human character. This change in the relation of man to his world implies that all reality has now become historical for him. All that is real for us after this change is that which we are able to understand historically. And this means that metaphysical thinking has lost its position of dominance. History is now no longer, as it was for the medieval theology of history, 'a process within a stationary—that is to say a metaphysically conceived—world'. 'On the contrary, the world and the entire relation of man to it have now become part of history. It is not the world which is the all-embracing problem, but history.'[2]

Two points require consideration here. First the fact that this total historicization (*Vergeschichtlichung*) of human existence is not merely something in the nature of a theory or one of the many *Weltanschauungen* which in one way or another can be

[1] Gerhard Krüger, *Die Geschichte im Denken der Gegenwart*, p. 17.
[2] Gerhard Krüger, *Die Geschichte im Denken der Gegenwart*, p. 14.

concocted to suit every taste. Rather one might say that it is
perceived to be the original condition of human existence, in
which we all live, Christians and non-Christians alike, and in
which this human existence consists by virtue of being everyday constituted and reaffirmed by our factual thinking and
action. The second matter which must be considered with
regard to this historicization of human existence is the question
of its origin. At this juncture it must be stated that history,
in the sense in which it is still generally understood, came into
being only with romanticism. It was in the thinking of the
romantics that the so-called 'historical sense' awoke, which
then led to modern historical and philosophical science and
within it to the elaboration of the 'critical historical method'.
This historical science is principally concerned with history in
so far as it is past or can at least be considered as being past, and
it is to the investigation of this that it applies the 'historical
method'. What is aimed at here is a detached attitude to history,
the attitude of a spectator who holds himself aloof from history,
or at any rate is under an obligation to hold himself as completely aloof from it as he can. It is, however, necessary to
draw a distinction between the approach to history which we
have just described and another approach which has been
scientifically developed in more recent times. According to this
latter view such an objective attitude is not possible because
the approach is itself historical. Of this interpretation it might
also be said that it is not primarily directed towards history
in the sense of past events but to present history, and not to
present history in the sense in which one attempts to understand
it in anticipation as what is past, but to present history understood as that which is still to occur.

To understand history in this way is to be aware of one's
responsibility for history, as that which is now to occur.

This view of history, of which the essence is the knowledge that one is responsible for history, is considerably older than the view of history developed in modern historical science, which is mainly a matter of historical investigation. And if we enquire after its origin it is not sufficient to point to the modern age and to the way in which in this modern age man with his rationally acquired knowledge has assumed responsibility for the historical form of the world and its ordering.[1] Of the particular form in which this awareness of responsibility has emerged in the course of the development of the modern period up to our own day it must be said that it is at the beginning of the modern period that it has its origin. But this is not true of the responsibility itself. The extraordinarily surprising and still scarcely heeded truth about this responsibility is, on the contrary, that it has its origin in the Christian faith.

This becomes evident at once if the relation of man to the world as it is understood by the Christian faith is compared with the attitude to the world assumed by pre-Christian man. Pre-Christian man 'lived, with the freedom which he more or less consciously possessed, in an inner subjection to powers which were superior to him, in other words in a religion'.[2] It must, however, be added here that this 'religion', seen from the point of view of the Christian faith, was distinguished by the fact that in it, as Paul expresses it in the first chapter of Romans, it was the creature and not the Creator which was the object of divine worship. The powers to which the man of pre-Christian antiquity knew himself to be subject were

[1] An excellent characterization of the way in which this took place at the beginning of the modern period is given by Dilthey in his description of the 'natural system of the philosophical sciences in the seventeenth century' (*Gesammelte Schriften*, Vol. II, pp. 90-245).

[2] Krüger, *Die Geschichte im Denken der Gegenwart*, p. 16.

therefore created powers, that is to say, powers pertaining to the world. Consequently it would be quite meaningless to say of this religion that it involved a responsibility of man for the world, and consequently real history. For the Christian faith the situation is basically different. This is evident from the fact that according to the Christian faith man's sin consists precisely in his reversing the fundamental order of all being by his worshipping of the creature instead of the Creator, so that, as Romans 8.19ff. expresses it, the creature has been made subject to vanity and corruption. That is why Paul can say that 'the earnest expectation of the creature waiteth for the manifestation of the sons of God', by whose liberty it is to be 'delivered from the bondage of corruption'. If one bears in mind what Paul says in Galatians 4 about the redemption of the believer to liberty and so to sonship and adulthood, it becomes evident that this filial freedom, being freedom for the Father, is at the same time freedom from the law and consequently freedom from that power with which the world is most powerfully enclosed within itself and with which the world holds man prisoner. And furthermore it becomes evident that man with this freedom, as the 'lord of all' who has now come of age, governs the world as his paternal heritage, and that the principal task which is entrusted to him, when he is given this lordship over the world, is to maintain the world in the worship of the Creator as the creature which it is. We may conclude from this that sin is the responsibility for the world in so far as the right to it has been forfeited but the obligation of it still remains, and that man's filial freedom, in its two meanings, in relation to God, and in relation to the world, is the fulfilment of this responsibility in faith.[1] Thus the responsibility

[1] Cf. Gogarten, *Der Mensch zwischen Gott und Welt* (especially the section entitled *Kultur*).

of man for the world, and with it the historical nature of human existence and of its world, has its basis in the Christian faith and in the historical nature of that faith.

It is therefore, actually because of this historical character of faith that the historical approach, which began in a still very superficial manner with an examination of the Bible as the means by which the word of God is transmitted, does not stop short at this but applies itself also to the Word itself, that is to say to the revelation and to the events of the revelation. It is by faith that the historical interpretation has been called into being and set in motion, and it is consequently faith also which has evoked the 'historical method'. We have already said that the 'historical method', however it may be handled, is an expression of the fact that modern man can interpret history and its reality only from the standpoint of his responsibility for the world and its conformation. Since this interpretation is a methodical one, it follows that it can exclude nothing from the range of this responsibility, neither the interpretation itself nor any reality which has to be interpreted.

Certainly the question now arises whether historical interpretation as it is practised in the modern historical approach is still genuinely historical. We have already indicated that in considering this responsibility for the world, which is what history is about, one must distinguish between this responsibility as such and the particular way in which it is understood. It is true that Christian faith and the responsibility which it discloses are the origin of that responsibility for the form of the world which modern man has taken upon himself with his science, culture and technology, and which by rendering his existence as well as his world historical has made history the one problem for him which embraces the whole of reality. But this does not by any means answer the question whether the particular way in which modern man understands his responsibility has the same origin. It is therefore in fact still necessary to enquire whether the historical interpretation as it is practised in the modern historical approach has retained its historical character in accordance with its origin. And this involves the question whether the 'historical method' is still a critical one. To say that the 'historical method' is a critical method does not by any means, as is generally supposed, imply only that it criticizes the tradition. It implies first and foremost that it is critical of itself in assessing its own conformity to history. It is in conformity with history, or, as we may also say, it remains historical, only if it has the power to compel the questioning and thinking which it governs to remain open to history till the end and consequently to prevent it from escaping from historical reality and taking refuge in the metaphysical reality which claims to be antecedent and superior to all history and therefore, since human responsibility cannot but be historical, to all human responsibility.

If the turning-point between the metaphysical thought of the middle ages and the historical thought of the modern period comes, as Dilthey expresses it in the passage which we have already quoted, when 'the motives of the movement of history are sought for within humanity itself', then it must be asked what modern historical thought understands by this. Dilthey himself, who may surely be regarded as a representative exponent of this modern historical thought, quite clearly refers it to that movement of ideas, beginning in the sixteenth century, which considers 'the creative nature of man to be the source of knowledge and consequently of all the achievements of the mind' and which 'endeavours to go back behind the traditional formulations, histories and dogmas to something humanly divine which is always and everywhere active in the soul and of which all these particular manifestations of religious life are products'. He says of this movement of ideas that it is present in the thought of 'Denck and Franck, Coornheert and Bodin, Valentin Weigel and Jacob Böhme, Kant and Goethe, Schleiermacher, Carlyle and Hegel. Its centre lies not in theology but in the great awareness of the creativeness and of the links with the unseen in man's nature, properties which manifest themselves in art, religion and morality as well as in philosophical speculation. The whole of history is its realm.'[1]

It is no doubt Troeltsch who, as a theologian troubled by the immensely difficult problem of the relation between faith and history, has studied the problem of history in its most comprehensive aspects. He was determined to be guided by his conviction that the real problems of history 'arise from the inner nature of history itself as soon as it has been consciously seen to be history' and that consequently it is only in the nature of history itself that a solution for these problems can be found. As a result of his detailed examination of historical thought he comes to the surprising conclusion that the key for the solution of the problems which this thought raises is 'the essential and individual identity of finite minds with the infinite mind, and, precisely through this, their intuitive participation in its concrete contents and its motivated vital unity'.[2] Even if one says, as Troeltsch does, that this identity of finite minds with the infinite can be 'only a very conditional one', it is still not difficult to perceive that modern historical thought, in taking over this idea as the solution for the problem of the philosophy of history which it involves and consequently also as the initial basis for its understanding of history, is in fact departing from history and seeking refuge in metaphysics. It thus robs of its

[1] Dilthey, *Gesammelte Schriften*, Vol. II, p. 109.
[2] Troeltsch, *Der Historismus und seine Probleme*, p. 109 and p. 677.

proper significance and force the realization that history is in itself the problem which embraces the whole of human reality, man's own reality as well as that of his world. And if, as we have said, this realization is the expression of the fact that man, with the 'historicization' of his existence and of his world, as it is originally disclosed in the Christian faith, has assumed responsibility for this existence and world, then it follows that this flight of modern historical thought into metaphysics implies that it is not standing up to the full ultimate weight of this responsibility.[1]

[1] Cf. Gogarten, *Verhängnis und Hoffnung der Neuzeit. Die Säkularisierung als theologisches Problem* (*The Bane and the Hope of the Modern Age. Secularization as a Theological Problem*)

VI

The Supersession of Metaphysical by Historical Thought

IF it is true to say that modern historical thought, contrary to its own premises, returns a metaphysical and not a historical answer to the question which is always inseparable from the concept of history, the question of its totality and unity and consequently of its origin and purpose, then it is easy to see that it cannot satisfy the requirements of the historical character (*Geschichtlichkeit*) of the Christian faith. And whenever this historical thought has not confined itself to research conducted so to speak along purely technical lines with the sole purpose, as one might also say, of cataloguing for the sake of antiquarian interest the store of available ideas and concepts of the Christian tradition; whenever it has set out to achieve an understanding of the Christian faith itself which this tradition conveys, it has allowed itself to be guided by its conception of 'the humanly divine element which is always and everywhere at work in the human soul and which produces all the forms of the religious life' and it has consequently regarded the Christian faith as simply one of these forms, perhaps the most perfect so far. Or, to use the phrase in which Troeltsch expresses the same idea, 'it has translated it in terms of general rational truths which find in it their historical embodiment as the climax or as a transitional stage of their development, and which continue to operate on the basis of the faith with a constant refinement of their rational content'.[1] It is easy to see that not very much remains of the faith after this 'translation' to which this historical approach subjects it in order to 'understand' it, a translation of its historical content into a suprahistorical truth. At any rate such an interpretation eliminates precisely that which is the 'object' of the New Testament, namely what takes place between God and Christ and the world, and if in this 'translation', as Troeltsch no doubt quite rightly calls it, so-called Neo-Protestantism regards the old Church dogma as 'finally dead' and consequently does not go back to 'the biblical roots of the dogma, the Pauline-Johannine christology', but rather to 'the person and teaching of Jesus'; and if from this vantage point it re-surveys the world of ideas of Christianity, subordinating to it and freely incorporating in it the remaining elements of truth in the dogma,[2] then it is perfectly clear that this historical view of the Christian faith has the remarkable effect that the history which is the 'object' of this faith, the events taking place between God and man, is transformed into a body of ideas. For this is to go back to Jesus, His person and doctrine, in accordance with the notion already described of the 'humanly divine element everywhere and always active in the soul of man', an element which in Him, as one of the 'founders and heroes' of the religious life, was particularly pure and powerful.[3]

This consequence of the historical interpretation of the Christian faith cannot satisfy a theology which is conscious of its task of taking as its 'object' the gospel of Jesus Christ as it is evidenced in the New Testament. But what is this theology

[1] *Protestantisches Christentum und Kirche in der Neuzeit* (*Protestant Christianity and the Church in Modern Times*), p. 698.

[2] Troeltsch, *Protestantisches Christentum und Kirche*, p. 687f.

[3] Troeltsch, *Protestantisches Christentum und Kirche*, p. 698.

to do? One course is certainly not open to it today. It cannot dispense with the historical approach. It can dispense neither with its critical historical techniques of investigation as they are applied to the historical tradition of the Christian faith nor with the historical approach to the faith itself or to the revelation upon which the faith knows itself to be founded. Theology can therefore no longer return to the metaphysical view which assumed its classical form in the old Church dogma. This metaphysical view was possible only so long as it comprised in the same manner not only the faith and the eternal divine reality which goes with it but also the temporal terrestrial reality of man. So long as that is the case, the mystery of the revelation, in which there took place the miracle of the union of the divine nature with human nature, can be re-enacted at any time or place in sensible substantial presence. For just as in the incarnate Son of God the divine nature permeates and dominates human nature, so too does the Church which the incarnate God has founded permeate and dominate the entire earthly world. She can do this because as the mystical body of Christ, the *corpus Christi mysticum*, in her own essence she consists in the unity of the divine and human nature. In the sacraments, which are founded upon this unity, and in the veneration of saints and relics, she imparts the power of the divine to the earthly in the natural element and takes up the earthly into her own human-divine nature. But as soon as this metaphysical thinking is superseded by historical thinking, even if this historical thinking is at first applicable only to earthly events, the metaphysical and sacramental unity of the supernatural with the natural is broken and the revelation with its metaphysical unity of the divine nature with human nature is isolated from earthly matters by a gulf which no theological artifice can bridge, so that belief in this isolated revelation is now possible only by dint of an arbitrary resolution, a situation from which it can never again escape.

Once the metaphysical interpretation of the faith has been rendered impossible by historical thought, theology can only interpret the faith historically. We have already spoken of one possible historical approach and seen that it leads to the disintegration of the faith. Two other possibilities remain. They may be described in a rough and ready manner as follows. In both cases one starts, as one practically must do when one undertakes a historical interpretation of the faith and of the revelation which underlies it, from the hypothesis that what is spoken of in the New Testament is quite certainly the historical events upon which the Christian faith is based, especially the history of Jesus Christ taking place in His birth, His earthly life, His proclamation of His message, and His crucifixion and resurrection. This one approach sees its primary task in the establishment of the authenticity of this history in what it usually calls its 'objective' historicity, its 'real factualness', because, it maintains, this is the only way of preserving the 'trans-subjective' reality of the faith. Here, for this approach, lies the crucial theological decision. All other questions are secondary and must be formulated and directed in accordance with what has here been decided. History is understood here primarily as referring to past events and the task of the historian is taken to be the reconstruction of the past on the basis of documentary tradition. The other view differs from this one in that it arises from the conviction that the actual history—and, one must add, the actual historical character (*Geschichtlichkeit*)—of the events recorded in the New Testament is not to be sought in the 'objective' and historically (*historisch*) ascertainable fact of their having taken place, but in the *kerygma*, the proclamation and witness that in the events of

37

this history God turns with grace towards mankind and their world. If one separates the history of Jesus Christ from this proclamation in which alone it is transmitted to us, then, it is maintained, one is losing precisely the history upon which everything depends because without it there can be no genuine —that is to say justifying—faith. It follows from this view that not only past history is history, and that the task which history sets is not merely to investigate past events, reconstructing them and ascertaining the 'objective' fact of their having occurred. Whenever one is concerned with history one is concerned also with the historical character (*Geschichtlichkeit*) of human existence. For without this there could be no such thing as history. And since this means that the historical character of human existence is involved in every approach to history and desires to reach understanding, it follows that the study of history has not yet achieved its purpose when it has completed its investigative work of reconstructing and establishing the historical facts of the past but that this purpose is fulfilled only with the historical interpretation of these facts as a possibility of human existence. The investigation is not an end in itself but a means to this interpretation.

These two possible interpretations of the Christian faith and of the events which underlie it are the topic under discussion in the so-called demythologization controversy. Both parties are concerned with the understanding of history, but their approaches are so fundamentally different that each thinks itself obliged to deny that the opposing interpretation of history is genuine. It is therefore necessary for us to examine these two views more closely.

VII

The Historical View of the Faith in the 'Official' Theology of the Church

FOR the first of these theories, as we have said already, everything depends on the 'objective historicity' of the events of the revelation. This is broadly speaking the view held by the governing bodies of the Churches and the theologians associated with them. The crucial difficulty with this theory is that on the one hand it affirms this 'historical factualness', by which it means the same sort of historicity as historical science generally predicates of the occurrences it establishes, while on the other hand it must at the same time assert that these events, since they are after all the 'redemptive acts of God', 'are entirely without analogy and cannot be grasped by human thought'.[1] It is therefore necessary to make such contradictory statements about these events as, for example, that they 'are quite simply suprahistorical but are occurrences which break into history and show themselves within it'.[2] And then it is said that 'with this history of God the end of history is on the way in'. And although 'this history of God is something which can be assigned to a definite position in

[1] Eduard Ellwein, *Fragen zu Bultmanns Interpretation des neutestamentlichen Kerygmas* in *Ein Wort lutherischer Theologie zur Entmythologisierung*, ed. Ernst Kinder, Munich, 1952, p. 26.

[2] Ellwein in *Ein Wort lutherischer Theologie*, p. 26.

history, yet in its actual essence it is an event which is not historically comprehensible'.[1] Or again, it is asserted that 'the events', the facts of this history, are 'real in the sense of objective occurrence', and yet they are 'realities which cannot be established by historical means'.[2] If these are not to be the most crass contradictions it must be assumed that such assertions about the reality of these historical events imply a distinction between two strata, a stratum which 'breaks into history and shows itself within it' and a 'suprahistorical' stratum, a distinction between something which 'can be assigned to a definite place in history' and the 'actual essence' of this reality which is itself 'not historically comprehensible', or between reality 'in the sense of objective occurrence' and a reality which 'cannot be established by historical means'. If such a distinction is drawn, then one would expect faith to be directed to the 'suprahistorical' reality, the reality which cannot be ascertained historically. And in fact many statements are made which point in this direction. For example: 'It is certainly correct to say that the objective factualness of these redemptive occurrences cannot as such be the basis of faith'.[3] Or again, referring to the miracles of Jesus and the events on Calvary: 'Actual knowledge of such occurrences as revelation of God is accessible only to faith'.[4] But it would be a mistake to suppose that these statements are intended to imply the abandonment of the 'objective factualness' of the 'objects' of belief, i.e. of these very occurrences. For in spite of the distinction which is drawn here between the two strata of reality in the redemptive occurrences this would in fact be depriving the revelation of its historical

[1] Ellwein, in *Ein Wort lutherischer Theologie*, p. 18.
[2] Ernst Kinder, *Historische Kritik und Entmythologisierung*, in *Ein Wort lutherischer Theologie*, p. 49.
[3] Kinder in *Ein Wort lutherischer Theologie*, p. 48.
[4] Künneth in *Ein Wort lutherischer Theologie*, p. 80.

character. For, if language is still to have any meaning, whatever is 'suprahistorical' or 'historically incomprehensible reality' is quite certainly not history. But it is of the utmost importance for the view of the faith of which we are speaking here that the faith, and especially that in which the faith believes, should be understood historically. Consequently these assertions are not at all intended to imply that the 'objective historicity' of the events of the revelation is to be relegated to the background. On the contrary, they are intended to show that it is with these 'objective' occurrences that the faith is concerned. For even if these occurrences 'as such' 'cannot be the basis of the faith', that is still no reason for dispensing with the principle of 'objective factualness'.[1] With such a 'relativization of history' one would 'fail to grasp the essence and the unique character of the biblical historical faith and to discern the foundations of belief, namely the revelation which is inseparable from history'.[2] This means then that in the redemptive history a distinction must be drawn between the 'objective' occurrences in it which 'can be assigned to a definite place in history' and their 'historically incomprehensible actual essence'. But it does not mean that these may be separated from one another. For precisely this would be to fail to grasp the peculiar character of the faith, namely that in the facts of the redemptive history which have 'entered into our creaturehood and history' as 'real events' it discerns a 'claim to reality which is *sui generis*', a claim not only to the 'suprahistorical' reality of which we have heard so much but a claim also to be 'the way which somehow or other leads to *all* reality', since what has happened here, that is to say in the redemptive history, claims not only to be a reality among other realities but to be the

[1] Kinder in *Ein Wort lutherischer Theologie*, p. 48.
[2] Künneth in *Ein Wort lutherischer Theologie*, p. 80.

reality of all reality! Consequently it now has to be compared and contrasted with natural reality. In such a comparison, which is indispensable if the Incarnation is to be taken seriously, the realities of the 'redemptive history' too must not be dialectically exempted from historical criticism but in one way or another they must accept it willy-nilly.[1] What this 'one way or another' and this 'willy-nilly acceptance of historical criticism' involve becomes clear enough in the remark that this history and its reality 'must on principle, not only as regards their application but also as regards their being, be entirely free from the tyrannical chaperonage of the historical, but that nevertheless *a posteriori* they must not fight shy of historical criticism or seek exemption from it'.[2] Now this of course, as Troeltsch once said in a similar discussion, is 'setting problems like mousetraps',[3] and the historian whose criticism is being asked for here is not to be envied. If he accepts the idea of judging as a historian, whatever line he may take he will be rendering himself guilty of 'tyrannical chaperonage'. If he wishes to remain a historian all he will be able to say is that really he is not at all competent to speak on this point since the reality on which he is asked to pass judgment is not history either way—either as 'suprahistorical' reality or as 'natural' reality—even if the 'suprahistorical' reality is the reality of all realities.

I have already said that the difficulty with this view lies in the fact that it asserts not only that the redemptive events are 'objectively factual' and therefore 'assignable to a definite place in history' but also that they 'cannot be conceived by human thought' and are 'accessible only to faith'. The question which must be clarified before one can go any further is

[1] Kinder in *Ein Wort lutherischer Theologie*, p. 52.
[2] Kinder in *Ein Wort lutherischer Theologie*, p. 50.
[3] *Absolutheit des Christentums*, p. xxiii.

therefore this: How can this 'objective reality' be combined with 'the reality which cannot be established by historical means' in such a way that they are one and the same? How, in other words, can one speak of a revelation which is 'inseparable from history', or how can one say that 'revelation is always more than history, not only history but not without history'.[1] But no sort of answer is given to this question. The mere assertion that it is so does not help. The question is perhaps touched on but certainly not answered when reference is made to 'the entry of the revelation of God into history, into the time and space pattern and into the linguistic structure of the world'. And it is still not answered when it is added that 'revelation' shapes history as a 'sign' and involves history in the 'redemptive process'.[2] What *is* 'a sheer suprahistorical event which nevertheless breaks in into history'?

A certain sense can be found in all these assertions only if it is realized that unconsciously and probably involuntarily the argument is based on the metaphysical interpretation of the faith to which we have already referred. The only difference is that in the former case it was a question of human and divine nature, of the natural and the supernatural, whereas here it is a question of the historical and the suprahistorical. One can now no longer speak of the natural and the supernatural but only of history because since historical thought rose to its present predominance no reality has been of any concern to us unless it is historical. Consequently the reason now given for 'subjecting the Bible to historical and literary critical study' is that 'in this way the Bible's character of reality is taken seriously and seen in a clearer light'.[3] This 'character of reality'

---

[1] Künneth in *Ein Wort lutherischer Theologie*, p. 80.
[2] Künneth in *Ein Wort lutherischer Theologie*, p. 80.
[3] Kinder in *Ein Wort lutherischer Theologie*, p. 33.

of the Bible consists precisely in the fact that it records history. And because that is so the metaphysical system is not taken over unchanged. In the metaphysical view of the faith the guiding concept which embraced the whole of reality, both natural and supernatural, was the concept of a metaphysical hierarchy of being, and, made possible by this, the concept of the sacrament, this latter a concept which in itself brings about the unification of the natural with the supernatural and of the terrestrial and human with the divine. The place which in the metaphysical system was occupied by the natural is now given to history. In making this change no attention whatever is paid to what it really means or to the consequences which must follow from it. History is here defined in accordance with the idea that the task of historical investigation is to reconstruct the past by means of a critical examination of the tradition. History, understood in this way, is concerned essentially with what has happened, that is to say with the 'historical facts'. No less an authority than Leopold von Ranke is cited in support of the view that history 'can do no more than ask: What is recorded by tradition? What is asserted? What is believed?' While on the other hand history 'can neither prove nor contest the reality of the redemptive revelation'.[1]

But now the question is how these historical facts can be unified with the suprahistorical reality. For it is only by this unification that these facts acquire a redemptive-historical meaning and become 'redemptive facts', and conversely it is only by this unification that the historical character of the redemptive history and with it the 'objectively real character of reality' of the objects of faith can be established. To assert the unity of these two things, the historical and the supra-historical, leads to intolerable contradictions. It involves a

[1] Künneth in *Ein Wort lutherischer Theologie*, p. 80.

requirement which is meaningless because it simply cannot be fulfilled, namely that these objects of faith 'must on principle be free from the tyrannical chaperonage of the historical but must nevertheless not *a posteriori* fight shy of historical criticism or seek exemption from it'.[1] It is not at all surprising, then, if faith fails to fulfil its obligation when it is called upon to accept the unity of the historical with the suprahistorical in place of what was demanded of it by the metaphysical interpretation of the revelation, the sacrament effective *ex opere operato*, i.e. by virtue of its 'objective' consummation. Indeed it could accept this unity only if it were itself founded upon it. But in this scheme of things that is not at all the case, and indeed the basis of faith is the subject of the most extremely contradictory assertions. For on the one side we are assured that 'faith, as faith, knows itself to be motivated, supported and substantiated by facts',[2] and on the other side it is maintained that 'it is certainly correct to say that the objective factualness of these objective occurrences cannot as such be the basis of faith'.[3] If both these assertions are made it is not because of arbitrary or inconsequential thinking but because neither can be avoided although the two are mutually exclusive. The first assertion is necessary because in accordance with the view of history by which this theory is governed this is the only way of preserving the historical character of the faith and with it that 'objective reality' which is thought to be indispensable to it if it is to be faith in the New Testament sense, since it is held that in the New Testament 'the fact is the primary prerequisite of which faith is the secondary consequence'.[4] And the second assertion is necessary because without

[1] Kinder in *Ein Wort lutherischer Theologie*, p. 50.
[2] Kinder in *Ein Wort lutherischer Theologie*, p. 51.
[3] Kinder in *Ein Wort lutherischer Theologie*, p. 48.
[4] Künneth in *Ein Wort lutherischer Theologie*, p. 79.

it faith would be merely a matter of considering the fact to be true.

One must not, however, overlook the circumstance that the first of these assertions which we have just quoted probably does not refer to the 'facts' in their pure 'objective factualness' but that a factualness of a particular kind is intended, namely a 'supernatural reality' which, independently of faith, has given rise to faith as such and which 'only faith indeed, as faith, perceives and recognizes in its objective factualness, from which faith as faith draws its life and nourishment, but which for all that is still factual reality'. By this means, it is claimed, there is achieved among other things a 'genuinely theological concept of reality'.[1] Certainly it can be maintained that the concept of reality intended here is a theological one. But equally certainly it is genuine only for the metaphysical theology of the ancient Church, and not for an historical theology. We may be sure that it is not by chance that the term 'supernatural' is applied here to the reality for which faith possesses a 'reality-sensorium and reality-criterion *sui generis*'. This concept of the 'supernatural' belongs to the metaphysical interpretation of the faith, and there it has a good meaning of its own. That is why here, when the reference is to historical reality, it appears shame-facedly between inverted commas.[2] But in this question of the reality upon which the faith is founded it is not permissible to swing to and fro as one pleases, speaking at one moment of history and at the next of the natural and the supernatural. A

[1] Kinder in *Ein Wort lutherischer Theologie*, p. 50.

[2] The concept of 'suprahistorical' reality, which is used as an alternative to this one, also points in the same direction. As is well known, it dates from the Enlightenment, which regarded the historical as the realm of the fortuitous, so that there could only be truth 'above' it. It is not difficult to see that this concept of the suprahistorical is nothing but the rationalization of the concept of the supernatural which was taken over from the old metaphysics.

decision must be made here between historical and metaphysical thought. Once one has begun to think historically—and we have seen that for the reasons which we have described theology can no longer do otherwise—then one must also think in historical terms of the reality with which faith is concerned and for which faith certainly possesses something in the nature of a reality-sensorium and reality-criterion. But this is very far from being accomplished by simply calling this reality a suprahistorical one. By this all too easy approach one can indeed define the problem involved, but one cannot solve it.

VIII

The Historical View of the Faith
in the
'Theology of Demythologization'

WE will now try to describe the other view of history, the one involved in the theology which accepts the Bultmann scheme for the demythologization, or, to express it in positive terms, for the existential interpretation of the New Testament. In undertaking this we shall do well to direct our attention to the question to which no answer could be provided by the view of history to which we have just referred. We must ask, that is to say, whether, according to this other interpretation, the unity of the divine and the human reality is an event in history and, if so, in what way this occurs. This conception of history is considerably more difficult to understand because it involves lines of thought which have not yet been fully explored and consequently brings with it a set of concepts to which in our ordinary thinking we are unaccustomed. The problem for which a solution is being sought here consists in defining in historical terms that reality which in the other theory, where it is conceived to be 'supernatural' or 'suprahistorical', necessarily remains outside history. Perhaps it is not superfluous if we point out once again at this juncture that this is not a problem which is arbitrarily introduced merely for the purpose of 'completing the pattern of a fashionable philosophy'.[1] For it is the Christian faith which confronts us with the problem of

[1] Kinder in *Ein Wort lutherischer Theologie*, p. 55.

history in the radical sense in which it concerns us today, since human existence, not only in its earthly and worldly aspect but also in its meaning in relation to God, is shown by the Christian faith to be historical.

Already in our brief outline of it we mentioned that in this new historical approach the concept of history is referred particularly to the historical character of human existence, and not principally, let alone exclusively, to the history of the past. We have also said already that although this view of history has only recently been subjected to a process of explicit conceptual clarification in philosophy and theology it is nevertheless older than that which is customary in modern historical thought and it has its origin in the Christian faith. For in this faith man recognizes himself to be responsible for the form of the world. His sin is the cause of the world's disorder. But in his freedom, which is disclosed to him in faith, his freedom as a son of God, the world has obtained the promise that it shall be delivered from the bondage of vanity and corruption and be restored as God's creation (Rom. 8.19ff.). It goes without saying that if we speak here of responsibility and accountability this concept is to be understood at the level of being and not only at the level of doing, just as is the case with the New Testament concept of sin and of freedom or righteousness. That is to say that, just like these New Testament concepts, the concept of responsibility too is not to be understood in terms of morals. Just as sin means man's being in, or, according to St. John, of, the world which by his guilt is made subject to vanity, and just as righteousness means being in and of and to Christ through whom man and with him the world is delivered from sin and from the power of death, so too must the concept of reality be understood to refer to the being of man, if we employ this concept here in order to interpret the historical character of human existence which the Christian faith discloses. And indeed even in its original literal meaning the term 'responsibility' (*Verantwortung*) does not denote a detached, arbitrary, self-chosen attitude but rather a 'response' (*Antwort*) which is evoked by a given 'word' (*sponsio—Wort*) and which can be made only with the being of the respondent.

If we apply the term historical to man with reference to his responsibility, in this sense of the word, for the world and its form, then it is certainly evident that his relation to the world cannot be expressed in terms of subject and object, for the subject-object pattern is inextricably linked with the Cartesian view of the world and of reality. Any assertion of this kind would fundamentally misrepresent man's relation to the world, destroying the historical character both of the 'object', in this case the world, and of the 'subject', that is to say of man. For indeed any assertion made within this subject-object pattern inevitably rests on the hypothesis of an 'isolated subject'[1] and consequently of course also of an equally isolated object, and, whichever of these one may set out from, it is in neither case possible to restore the original relationship between the world and man.

Nor is it possible, so long as one conducts one's thinking within this subject-object pattern, to overcome the isolation of the two terms and to return to the principle that they are historical in character. Incidentally this enables us to understand why in the other conception of history which we have described, the view that history is an 'objective' reality, the unification of the historical with the suprahistorical remains an insoluble problem, why it is not possible to regard the faith

[1] Cf. Heidegger, *Sein und Zeit*, § 43. *Dasein, Weltlichkeit und Realität*, pp. 200ff.

in such a way that one may say that in it this unification takes place, and why one must instead go so far as to break up the unity of the faith itself, dividing it into 'taking cognizance' (*notitia*) and 'assent' (*assensus*). Once our thinking is caught up in this subject-object pattern, the only possible way to disentangle it is to seek a philosophical means by which the pattern can be overcome. It must be recognized that even the most emphatic affirmation is not of the slightest assistance. It does not help even if one tries to make it more convincing by a last ditch appeal to faith. Since our thinking, especially in the sciences, has been conducted in accordance with this pattern for the past three hundred years or so, the subject-object pattern cannot be overcome except by a very considerable effort, an effort which requires time. Consequently this is the one point at which it is vitally necessary to overcome the habits of thought which are referred to as 'modern', the one point at which theology must win for itself the scientific philosophical approach which is appropriate to it. And if it is correct to say that 'the latest change in the direction of the classical natural science of the nineteenth century, a change made necessary by the findings of modern research into atomic structure and energy . . . opens up unsuspected possibilities of making accessible to modern man some of the knowledge contained in the New Testament faith',[1] that is precisely because these findings have rendered untenable the subject-object scheme of thought which after all underlies not only the natural science but also and to an equal extent the theology of the nineteenth century, and really indeed not only the liberal, or as it now tends to be called, the liberalistic theology but also, as the [anti-demythologist symposium entitled *Ein*] *Wort lutherischer Theologie* makes abundantly clear, the theology which strictly

[1] Künneth in *Ein Wort lutherischer Theologie*, p. 76.

follows the official ecclesiastical line. A good deal of useless discussion could be avoided in theology today if it were recognized that a very large part of the misunderstanding and lack of understanding between the disputants arises from failure to see clearly the bearing which this subject-object pattern has on our thinking.[1]

In the view of history which is now to be described the historical character of human existence is expressed in the concept of a responsibility which can be fulfilled only with man's own being. This concept implies that man stands with respect to the world in a relation in which he stands originally, that is to say a relation in which he stands already and has always stood, and not a relation which he must establish only subsequently as an isolated subject, as was the case within the subject-object pattern of thought, by either proving or 'believing in' the reality of the world. 'World' does not of course refer here to the totality of the contents of the world but to that which man originally finds himself to be 'in' and 'of'. Formally speaking these prepositions are used here in the same way as the 'in' and the 'under' in Paul's saying that both Jews and Greeks, in other words all mankind, are 'under' sin and 'in' the law (Rom. 3.9, 19), which means that one is and always

[1] One could find in the philosophical work of Heidegger an explanation, instructive for a theologian because it refers him insistently to his proper theological task, of the reason why our thinking so easily falls into this subject-object pattern and why once it is in it it cannot easily escape. And even if it were really the case, as one of the authors of the *Wort lutherischer Theologie* opines, that Heidegger's philosophy is 'to be regarded merely as a kind of secularized Christianity, a residual product of originally Christian substance', an opinion which incidentally would be true enough if it were expressed in a less contemptuous form, even if this were the case, I think, the theologian should be ashamed rather than proud about it. Needless to say, this truth does not have to be learnt from Heidegger. If one thinks one can learn it better from another source, all well and good. But, in one way or another, learnt it must be.

has been in and under them. That 'sin' in a saying of this kind also means 'world' is apparent from the fact that it is said to 'reign' (Rom. 5.21), and to reign in such a way that the world thereby becomes its world, the world of sin, so that now 'being in sin' is the same as 'being in the world'. It is of course clear that one would be misunderstanding this 'being in' if one were to conceive it spatially in the sense in which one might say for example that paper is in a folder. What this 'being in' does imply, depending on what I am said to be in, is a definite possibility of existence for me. Thus the possibility of existence implied for me in 'being in the law' and 'being under sin' is the one in which my existence is ruled by the law and by sin, 'ruled' in the sense that, in the responsibility which is proper to it in this 'being in', my existence is 'called up' (*aufgerufen*) by the sin which accuses me. Consequently the possibility of existence for me, as I have it in this 'being in sin', consists in my having to render account of myself (*mich ver*ANTWORT*en*) to the sin which reigns over me and which exercises its rule in accusing me by means of the law. In this accusation I hear its summons (*Anruf*). Because the summons, the 'word' (WORT), of sin is a question about my existence, I can give my answer (*Ant*WORT) only with my existence, or, to express it differently, only with myself.

Needless to say, this analysis of 'being in' is not the only way in which this can be expressed. Another way is simply the confession of one's sin, and the existential reference to this sin will be nothing other than the confession of it. But if one wishes to explain to oneself or to others what is meant when one speaks of sin—and as a theologian one has to do that either in the lecture room or in the pulpit or in some cases in the course of one's pastoral duties—then one must do it in the form of intelligible concepts, and, since sin concerns man's being and not only his doing, this means that one must express it by reference to the existential structure of 'being in', as is also done, of course, by the Apostle Paul.[1] And since this 'being in' is, as we have seen, a responsible one, namely one which implies responsibility to that in which one is, and since there is no responsibility without one's knowing of it, and since that for which in this case responsibility is held is the being of him who is responsible, it follows that there is no such responsibility unless he who holds it has knowledge of this his being for which he is responsible, that is to say of himself, or, to express it differently, unless he understands himself with reference to the existence which is here made possible for him or disclosed to him. The mode of existence 'made possible' in the present case by 'being under sin' and 'being in the law' is that of perdition, and this is what gives its particular meaning, a meaning determined by sin and its reign, to this 'understanding of oneself', or, in other words, to this understanding of how to be oneself in this way.

This then is what is meant by the famous, or rather as one must say, notorious self-understanding or understanding of existence which comes up so frequently in the discussion about 'demythologization' and which gives rise to the innumerable misapprehensions that inevitably render this discussion hopelessly fruitless. These misapprehensions all arise from the fact that not only Bultmann's opponents but, occasionally even his friends and followers with an astonishing lack of

---

[1] Cf. Heidegger, *Sein und Zeit*, p. 180. 'If faith or philosophy (*Weltanschauung*) asserts propositions with regard to either of these (referring back to the *status corruptionis* and the *status integritatis*), and if it asserts propositions with regard to "being there" (*Dasein*, Heidegger's term for human existence) as "being in the world", then, if we assume that its assertions claim at the same time to be intelligible *conceptually*, it will be obliged to have recourse to the exhibited (*herausgestellt*) existential structures.'

caution transpose this self-understanding, together with the 'existential interpretation' which is associated with it, into the traditional subject-object scheme of thought which we have already discussed. From this it follows without any further consideration, and with the logical necessity which thought conducted within the subject-object pattern cannot avoid, that this self-understanding is transformed into an 'immanent content of consciousness' or some sort of 'subjective validity and interpretation'[1] or 'feeling for life'.[2] Terms like these naturally give rise to the suspicion that anyone who relies on this kind of self-understanding 'comes perilously near to auto-suggestion, self-deception and illusion'.[3] And there arises the conviction that, if the message proclaimed in the New Testament is interpreted in accordance with a self-understanding which is conceived in this way, it will be 'made subject to the idea of immanence' and that then 'the reality of Christ can no longer be presented as it should be, as a "counterpart" (Gegenüber) which transcends human existence'.[4] In short, when this self-understanding is transposed into the subject-object pattern, which indeed it has just overcome or at any rate is trying to overcome, it is thereby transformed into an extremely subjectivistic phenomenon of consciousness which as such has no bearing on reality whatever or which may indeed be said to dissolve reality within itself. Any assertions with regard to the proclamation in the New Testament, the kerygma, and its historical character and reality, will then likewise, if only because it is explicitly stated that they are not concerned with 'objective factualness', be transposed into this subjectivism and transformed into 'mere contents of

[1] Künneth in *Ein Wort lutherischer Theologie*, p. 79.
[2] Kinder in *Ein Wort lutherischer Theologie*, p. 51.
[3] Künneth in *Ein Wort lutherischer Theologie*, p. 88.
[4] Bishop D. Haug's letter to the clergy of Württemberg.

consciousness' which are 'without objective foundation'[1] and in which the 'objective facts of redemption' have always only 'the abstract existence of a purely conditional "as if" '.[2] So long as one conducts one's thinking naïvely and unsuspectingly within this subject-object framework, failing to notice that in doing this one is relying on a philosophoumenon which, in spite of its three hundred years of general acceptance, will certainly be sought for in vain in the New Testament, even in the passages which speak of the redemptive event having been seen and touched; and, failing for the same reason to notice at all that this talk about self-understanding, and with it the attempt to achieve an existential interpretation, are directed towards the overcoming of this subject-object thinking, so long too will this total incomprehension continue to assert itself and with it the probably quite unconscious tendency to regard the understanding of self and of existence as a subjectivistic phenomenon of consciousness.

What Bultmann's opponents have failed to grasp is that the existential philosophy is concerned with the attempt to achieve a new understanding of the essential nature of history and that consequently it is towards an understanding of the historical character of the New Testament revelation in accordance with this essential nature of history that Bultmann's 'existential interpretation' is directed. Indeed in their complacent devotion to tradition—a tradition which incidentally is not so old as they think, for it certainly does not go back as far as Luther and there are grounds for questioning whether it dates from before Descartes—it does not even occur to them that anything of this sort might be involved. Instead they understand *existential* either in the sense of existentialism or else in the sense of *existentiell*; and here Bultmann quite often comes in for some

---

[1] Künneth in *Ein Wort lutherischer Theologie*, p. 88.
[2] Kinder in *Ein Wort lutherischer Theologie*, p. 53.

praise, but only because of a misunderstanding. For with him the term *existentiell* has a considerably deeper and, if I may be allowed the word, more *existentiell* meaning than it has with them, since with them it does not get far beyond the level of the 'moral of the story'.

No success attended the various attempts to understand history, in its peculiar essential nature, which were undertaken during and after the time of the Enlightenment and of the idealists. Today, however, in the endeavour to achieve an 'existential interpretation' there is being prepared an understanding of history which as we have already indicated could be characterized by saying that an attempt is being made to extricate history from the subject-object pattern of thought. According to this view man would no longer be the subject which is confronted by history as an object. For indeed the knowledge which we owe to historicism is that man, however he may be defined, is himself historical. Consequently he cannot in any way take himself out of history, least of all by making himself the subject which envisages history as its object. If he does do this he fails to grasp both himself and history. Man then becomes 'that being (*Seiendes*) upon which all being (*Seiendes*) is based in the manner of its being (*Sein*) and of its truth. Man becomes the centre of reference of being (*Seiendes*) as such.' The being (*Sein*) of that which is (*Seiendes*) consists here in that 'since it is brought before man as that which is objective it is placed within the range of his decision and authority and is thus alone being (*seiend*)'.[1] To say that man is himself historical is to say, briefly, that he is in history from the outset; he has in history not only his existence but also, from the outset, his origin. Consequently the crucial problem of history, if it is understood in this way, is the

[1] Heidegger, *Holzwege*, pp. 81, 83.

57

problem of hermeneutics, that is to say the problem of an interpretation which approaches history not from outside but from within the historical character of human existence or, more precisely, from (what Heidegger calls) 'my' (*je mein*) historical character. The essence of the historical interpretation is, therefore, that in it man understands himself. Or, to express it differently, man understands himself in this interpretation according to the particular possibilities of human existence. This then is the meaning of that 'self-understanding' which is what is involved in the 'existential interpretation'.

We ought now to consider what justification if any there is for the suspicion which is repeatedly being voiced by theologians that the existential interpretation is nothing more or less than a modern *Weltanschauung*, and that the attempt to understand the New Testament message in terms of the concepts which this interpretation has elaborated must, therefore, necessarily lead to emptying it of its meaning or falsifying it by transforming it into just such another *Weltanschauung*. If it is correct to say that the purpose of the conceptual analysis of human existence which this philosophy undertakes is to comprehend the phenomenon of 'historical character' (*Geschichtlichkeit*) and history with an appropriate set of concepts, then the question arises whether in this undertaking one succeeds in keeping to a formal and conceptual clarification of what 'historical character' is or whether in fact a certain *weltanschaulich* view of history is the outcome.[1] It seems to me that two considerations must here be borne in mind. First, in every assertion it makes, this philosophy is opposed to the subject-object thinking which has achieved

---

[1] Unfortunately even among theologians it is necessary to note explicitly that such a question cannot be answered on the basis of what one may happen to have read about this philosophy in newspaper articles.

practically unquestioned dominance since the awakening of rationalism in the seventeenth century. That subject-object thinking may with some justification be called a *Weltanschauung*. But is it true to say that in opposing that pattern of thought the existential philosophy is trying to replace it by another *Weltanschauung*? It is argued that whenever the 'criteria and methods of allegedly universally valid "scientificness" (*Wissenschaftlichkeit*) are asserted as *a priori* and absolute', then one's thinking is already governed by a 'certain feeling for life (*Lebensgefühl*) and a certain *Weltanschauung*'. For 'there are no such things as purely formal and objectively neutral categories of understanding and interpretation. If they are detached from one association with particulars (*Sachgebundenheit*), then they exist in another.'[1] The second point to be considered is that the *Weltanschauung* would then be one which had selected as its governing principle the 'historical character' (*Geschichtlichkeit*) of human existence.

To begin with the question of history as *Weltanschauung*, we have already spoken of how the matter stands. It certainly would be something in the nature of a *Weltanschauung* if one were to apply the term *Weltanschauung* to an undertaking which posits an underlying principle in order to interpret as history the totality of the world, or of reality in so far as it concerns man, and in order therefore to interpret the existence of man as historical existence. But we have already seen what is the origin of the historical character which impinges on and entirely dominates the whole of human existence. In the Christian faith there is disclosed the totality of the historical character of human existence as assuredly as for the Christian faith sin is the power which dominates the entire existence of man and with it the totality of his world, so that this world

[1] Kinder, in *Ein Wort lutherischer Theologie*, p. 44.

can be called the world of sin, and as assuredly as man bears the
guilt of this reign of sin which perverts all human reality into
the disorder of its 'un-being' (*Un-Wesen*), as assuredly, that is
to say, as man is responsible for this guilt. We have also seen
how in the philosophy of history which is adapted to the
modern historical approach this responsibility changes into a
metaphysical theory of a 'human nature, creative and linked
with the unseen, which manifests itself in art, religion and
morality as well as in philosophical speculation' and whose
'realm is history'.[1] We pointed out in that connexion that this
implies the evasion of the actual weight of the historical
responsibility which is imposed upon man by the Christian
faith. We may also express this by saying that in this way the
responsibility is brought within the range of man's self-deter-
mination. It has become the responsibility of the man who is
responsible only to himself. And we may also say that this
change has been influenced by precisely that subject-object
pattern of thought of which we have just been speaking. For
indeed this 'creative human nature', which has 'all history as its
realm' in which to manifest—i.e. to objectify—itself, is identical
with that 'mere "inner" ' (*das 'blosse "Innere" '*) which, 'if in this
ontological orientation (that of the subject-object pattern) the
problem is posed "critically", is at first alone certainly "on
hand" (*vorhanden*)'.[2] What is new and of special importance
in the achievement of the existential philosophy with its
existential analysis is that in contrast to the traditional interpretation of history it removes from the range of man's
arbitrary choice his responsibility for the totality of himself and
for the totality of the world and thereby once more allows this
responsibility to be a genuine one. It does this because, in

[1] Dilthey, *Gesammelte Werke,* Vol. II, p. 109.
[2] Heidegger, *Sein und Zeit*, p. 206.

accordance with its interpretation of human existence as 'being in the world', it refers this responsibility to the 'call' (*Ruf*) which calls human existence to itself. For it is only with itself that human existence can respond to this 'call' to which it is responsible. We may therefore say that through this interpretation of history the responsibility is rediscovered as it is when through the Christian faith there is originally disclosed in it the historical character of human existence.

If one were to say of the existential philosophy that it is a *Weltanschauung* because it interprets man and the world by reference to their historical character, then one would have to say the same of the Christian faith. But quite apart from that, it is impossible to speak of a *Weltanschauung* in this connexion for the simple reason that nothing is farther from the mind of this philosophy than setting up some particular goal in the name of this 'historical character' (*Geschichtlichkeit*) or ascribing to this history some particular meaning or asserting that it is meaningless, as would be done by what we usually refer to as a *Weltanschauung*. What it aims at and what it achieves is something very much less ambitious and yet incomparably more important, namely nothing more or less than the conceptual clarification of the structure of human existence and its historical character. In other words, the existential philosophy would be a *Weltanschauung* if it were to set up some sort of 'material ideal of existence' and if it 'were to say to man: "This is how you are to exist!"; but what it does say to him is only: "You are to exist!"—or perhaps even that is an overstatement and it would be better to say that this philosophy shows man what is meant by existing. It shows him that human being differs from all other being in that it means existing, a being which is committed to its own responsibility and has to take itself over. It shows that man's existence attains to its proper character only in existing, in other words that it is always realized only in each particular concrete here and now. But it does not aim at achieving by *existential* analysis the *existentiell* understanding of the now and the here. It does not relieve man of this. On the contrary, it charges him with it.'[1] And if we have just said that through the interpretation of history worked out in the existential analysis of the existential philosophy there is rediscovered the responsibility as it is when through the Christian faith the historical character of human existence is originally disclosed in it, this refers solely to the existential or, as one might also say, to the formal structure and not at all to the *existentiell* application or contents of this philosophy.

What we have said here about the essential nature of history has already indicated the main point in our first consideration with regard to the suspicion that perhaps the existential interpretation of the message proclaimed in the New Testament must necessarily lead to the subordination of this message to the tutelage of a *Weltanschauung* which happens at the present time to be 'modern', a *Weltanschauung* which has arisen by way of reaction against the subject-object thinking that has dominated the thought of the past three centuries. But there are still several more things to be said about this which may make still clearer what Heidegger's philosophy understands to be the essential nature of history. In an essay on *The Time of the World Picture*[2] Heidegger tries to show that the 'world

[1] Bultmann, *Kerygma und Mythos*, II, Hamburg, 1952, pp. 192f. (Cf. *Kerygma and Myth*, S.P.C.K., 1953, pp. 193f., where the passage is made clearer by rendering *existentiell* as 'existential' and *existential* as 'existentialist'. In the context of a translation from Gogarten, however, these renderings would be misleading, since it is essential to his argument that he uses the word *existential* only in the 'formal' sense of Heidegger's *Existenzphilosophie* and he states explicitly that it is misunderstood if it is referred to *Existentialismus*. TRANSLATOR.)

[2] Die Zeit des Weltbildes, in *Holzwege*, Frankfurt, pp. 69ff.

picture'—and this means that the world becomes a picture—
is the essence of our time, the modern age, and of its thought.
There could not be a medieval or ancient world picture, he
says, because before the modern period 'the being (*Sein*) of
what is (*Seiendes*) never consists in its being brought before man
as that which is objective and in its being placed within the
range of his decision and authority so that it alone is being
(*seiend*),[1] 'The underlying process of the modern age,' says
Heidegger, 'is the conquest of the world as a picture.[2] The
world becomes a picture or image (*Bild*); it becomes an object,
that is to say something objective which man is able to con-
quer; or, as Heidegger expresses it, it becomes a 'product of
imaginative construction'.[3] And the reason for this is that 'the
whole essential nature of man changes in that it becomes a
subject'. The decisive event in the modern period since
Descartes, who reduced it to clear conceptual terms, is that
'man becomes that being (*Seiendes*) upon which all being
(*Seiendes*) is based in the manner of its being (*Seien*) and
of its truth'.[4] Thus it is 'by one and the same process that
the world becomes a picture, or, as we have just said, an
object, and that man becomes a *subjectum*[5] within "what is"
(*das Seiende*)'[6]

This transmutation of man into a subject has consequently
brought with it a profound and fateful change in his relation to
the world and to all that is (*das Seiende*), a change which is still
in operation today. The world, and indeed all that is, has

[1] Heidegger, Die Zeit des Weltbildes, p. 83.
[2] Heidegger, Die Zeit des Weltbildes, p. 87.
[3] *Gebild des vorstellenden Herstellens.*
[4] Heidegger, Die Zeit des Weltbildes, p. 81.
[5] Heidegger understands the word *subjectum* as the translation of the Greek
hypokeimenon. 'The word,' he says, 'denotes that which lies before one (*das
Vor-liegende*) and which as a basis collects everything upon itself.'
[6] Heidegger, Die Zeit des Weltbildes, p. 85.

thereby become the object which man envisages (*sich vorstellt*).[1]
Heidegger makes the meaning of this clear by drawing a
comparison with the middle ages and ancient Greece. 'For the
middle ages "what is" (*das Seiende*) is the *ens creatum*, that which
is created by the personal Creator God as the Supreme Cause.
Being (*Seiendes*) in this case means belonging to a definite level
of the order of created things and corresponding as something
caused to the creative cause (*analogia entis*).' And for the Greeks
'being (*Sein*) implies the perception (*Vernehmen*) of what is
(*das Seiende*), because it (*Sein*) demands and determines it.
"What is" is that which is opening and displaying itself as
"that which is present" (*das Anwesende*[2]) coming upon man as

---

[1] TRANSLATOR'S NOTE. Heidegger and his followers often make deliberate
use of untranslatable ambiguities. They use words which are intended to
convey simultaneously both a literal and a figurative meaning, and some-
times, in addition to the current connotations of these terms, an obsolete or
supposed etymological sense is introduced. These double meanings are
frequently but not always indicated by hyphens (e.g. *Unwesen*, disorder,
confusion, mischief; *Un-Wesen*, un-being, where 'un-' conveys a perjorative
as well as a negative sense. *Vorliegend*, proposed or submitted; *vor-liegend*,
lying before one). *Sich vorstellen* means literally 'place before oneself', but
the word is probably also intended to convey two of its conventional
figurative meanings, namely 'conceive' (*Vorstellung*, conception) and
'imagine' (with reference to the 'image' or *Bild*). *Bild* means picture but may
also imply some of the senses of *bilden* (form) and *Gebild* (structure).

[2] AUTHOR'S NOTE: Here and in the following passage the words *Anwesen*
and *anwesend* are to be understood verbally.

TRANSLATOR'S NOTE: The word 'present' is therefore to be taken in
the sense of the verbal adjective 'being present', and the word 'presence'
is to be taken in the sense of the verbal noun 'being present'. The
etymological meaning of *Anwesen* is 'being at', and in addition to its current
connotation of 'being present' (e.g. a dignitary at a function) it is here
intended to refer to Heidegger's private verb *wesen* which could be exactly
translated only by reviving the obsolete present forms corresponding to the
English past tense 'was—were'. Heidegger avoids the use of nouns, and
instead of persons and things he introduces masculine and neuter sub-
stantival participles (*der* and *das Anwesende*). When these forms occur in any
other case than the nominative or accusative singular it is left to the reader
to decide which gender is intended.

"him who is present" (*der Anwesende*), that is to say upon him who is himself opening himself to "that which is present" in perceiving it.'[1] But since Descartes 'conception (*Vortstellen*) is no longer perception of that which is present, to the "un-concealedness" (*Unverborgenheit*) of which perception itself pertains as a particular kind of presence (*Anwesen*) in relation to the unconcealed "that which is present". Conception is no longer "unconcealing oneself for . . ." (*das Sich-entbergen für . . .*). It is now "grasping of . . ." (*das Ergreifen und Begreifen von . . .*). It is no longer that which is present but the attack or seizure (*Angriff*) which predominates. . . . "What is" is no longer "what is present"; it is now that which only in the process of conception (*Vorstellen*) is "placed against" as that which is "ob-jective".'[2]

What has been said here about the 'perception of that which is present' (*das Vernehmen des Anwesenden*) would furthermore be misunderstood if one were to overlook the fact that it is not intended in the sense of a statement about the contents of that which is being present (*was anwest*). Once again the assertions made here are on the contrary only formal ones relating to that which is and to the appropriate attitude (*Verhalten*) to it, the only attitude in which one allows it in its unconcealedness (*Unverborgenheit*—Heidegger's etymologizing translation of *aletheia*, truth) to be what it is, namely the being which un-conceals itself as that which is present (*das sich als das Anwesende ent-bergende Seiende*). And what is in this way true in general of 'what is' (*vom Seienden*) is true also of history (*Geschichte*) or of that which is historical (*geschichtlich*) and of the understanding of it. On this basis we may attempt to make clear what takes place in the existential interpretation of the New

---

1 Heidegger, Die Zeit des Weltbildes, p. 83.
2 Heidegger, Die Zeit des Weltbildes, p. 100.

Testament and what meaning this interpretation attaches to the historical character (*Geschichtlichkeit*) of the New Testament message.

Where the so-called 'theology of demythologization' has provoked the strongest disagreement is no doubt in its assertion that 'Christ the Crucified and Risen One comes before us in the Word of the proclaimed message and nowhere else. Nothing other than faith in this Word is in truth the Easter faith.'[1] This assertion was unhesitatingly taken to mean that in the Christian faith 'one is strictly speaking no longer concerned with the reality of the person of Jesus Christ which became present (*gegenwärtig*) in the kerygma but the kerygma itself actually usurps the place of the person of Christ'.[2] And again 'this kerygma, into which we are told Jesus rose and in which he therefore continues to live, allegedly came into being in the earliest Church (*Urgemeinde*) after the death of Jesus since this earliest Church at that time expressed the significance of this Jesus by means of myth'.[3] It is consequently asked with dismay whether in this way the history of God is perhaps 'so much curtailed and so entirely reduced to the act of belief (*Glaubensakt*), so completely involved and assimilated in the event of the proclamation of the message, so thoroughly transferred to the hearing and believing subject and enclosed within this subject, that it practically vanishes in it or alternatively exists only in it and only in this manner'.[4] From this there follows the conviction that this theology is open to the reproach that when it 'speaks of the Cross and of the Resurrection these are not redemptive facts (*Heilsfakta*) of a history which has taken place

[1] Bultmann, *Kerygma und Mythos*, I, p. 50 (Cf. *Kerygma and Myth*, S.P.C.K., 1953, p. 41.)
[2] Bishop D. Haug, *Brief an die württembergischen Pfarrer*, p. 5.
[3] *Ibid.*, p. 4.
[4] Ellwein, in *Ein Wort lutherischer Theologie*, p. 20.

but an interpretation of processes of consciousness in man'.[1]

This in its many variations is the objection which is repeatedly being raised against the new theological approach. If it were justified it would certainly be conclusive, if only because it would then show that this theology defeats its own purpose, which is to grasp the Christian faith once more in its original historical character, to allow it to be historical so that it once more enables the history of God to be what it is, and thus enables this history to take place in itself (*an sich*) instead of conceiving it (*sich vorstellen*) in accordance with the subject-object pattern. For indeed that is the meaning and purpose of demythologization—to interpret the mythical form (*Gestalt*), which is found in a number of formulations (central ones) in the New Testament message, in such a way that the history is perceived to which alone they are intended to bear witness— as is extremely clearly shown by the various particular contexts in which they appear and by the New Testament message as a whole. And when one of the authors of *Ein Wort lutherischer Theologie* opines that if his reading of Bultmann is correct Bultmann's 'first concern is not for demythologization but for dehistoricization',[2] one can only reply that his reading of Bultmann is a very superficial one.

It is simply not understood what is in question in the controversy to which the 'demythologization programme' has given rise. One cannot make the slightest contribution to the clarification of the discussion, and still less to the settlement of it, if one fails to see that the question in dispute between the two parties is not whether the great acts of God 'are set before all human existence, indestructibly, indissolubly and irremovably'.[3] For this is affirmed by both sides, and indeed

---

[1] Künneth in *Ein Wort lutherischer Theologie*, p. 83.

[2] Schieder, *ibid.* p. 93.   [3] Ellwein, *ibid.* p. 28.

with no less determination by the 'demythologizing' party than by their opponents. The question in debate, the question which must therefore be decided, is rather, how—in what way —the history of God precedes all the being and doing of man. On the one side it is asserted that it is in the way of 'objective factualness', while on the other side it is asserted that since God's action takes place in the destiny of a concrete historical man and is accordingly a unique historical event it comes before man as that which is set before his existence in the *kerygma* of the New Testament.

Our task must now be to show whether and, if so, how this *kerygma* has the character not only of history but of a history which is in every sense 'indestructibly, indissolubly and irremovably set before' all human existence. To formulate it briefly, this is the question of whether it is really true to say that in the existential interpretation of the New Testament message 'the bridge between the historical Jesus and the preached Jesus has so to speak collapsed'.[1]

We will begin by asking what is meant by the word *kerygma*. It is the proclamation or announcement of a herald (in Greek *keryx*). This herald does not make his proclamation on his own authority, but on behalf of someone else whose herald he is. It is in this way that Jesus in the synoptic gospels is the proclaimer of the kingdom of God, that is to say He is God's herald. Moreover the meaning of His proclamation is not, as it was in the case of John the Baptist, 'that something will happen, but his *kerygma* is already a happening; at the moment of its announcement what is announced becomes reality'.[2] Just as the Word of Jesus is the Word of God, so that whoever hears Him hears God, so too therefore is the proclamation of

[1] Ellwein in *Ein Wort lutherischer Theologie*, p. 23.
[2] *Theologisches Wörterbuch zum Neuen Testament*, Vol. III, p. 705.

those whom Jesus sends as His messengers His own proclamation, so that it can be said of them that 'he that heareth you heareth me' (Luke 10.16). It is already clear from what we have said so far about the *kerygma* that it is not—or at any rate not primarily—intended to be a kind of report about something that has happened, for after all a reporter is not a herald. It is rather a kind of declaration of the sender's will, addressed to and intended for the particular person to whom the herald is sent. This would still be the case if something which has happened were to be reported in the herald's message. This happening would then be of such a kind as to refer to him for whom the herald's message is intended. If in considering the *kerygma* with which we are here concerned we bear in mind from whom the proclamation originates there follows a further conclusion which has a very important bearing on our assessment of its character. It is God who sends Jesus as His messenger into the world. That is why in Mark and Luke Jesus' proclamation is spoken of as *keryssein*. The contents of His message is the salvation which God has prepared for mankind. And this salvation is God Himself, in His turning Himself as God towards mankind, as He does precisely in this proclamation of Jesus, because the Word of Jesus is the Word of God.

If we really want to know what the New Testament *kerygma* is all about, then we cannot very well do otherwise than ask what is meant by saying that the Word of Jesus is the Word of God. It obviously means something different from what it means when we say the same thing of the Old Testament prophets or of John the Baptist. Certainly their message too speaks of God turning towards His people, but it tells either how God turned towards the patriarchs or how He will turn towards His people in the future, and it is only in this indirect sense that it can be said of this message too that 'salvation takes place within it'. In the proclamation of Jesus, on the other hand, the turning of God towards man takes place directly, once and for all and it is this event which is meant in that which was vouchsafed to the patriarchs as well as in that which was promised for the future. We may say then first of all that when it is asserted that the Word of Jesus is the Word of God this means that in this Word, by Jesus' speaking it, the same thing happens as happens if God speaks—just as it is said of Jesus's appearance in the synagogue of Nazareth that 'this day is this scripture fulfilled in your ears' (Luke 4.21). But with this something has been said about the relation of Jesus to God which seems to go beyond what has been said about the Word of Jesus. What has been asserted is a unity between God and Jesus which does not extend only to the Word which Jesus speaks. What kind of unity is this?

In view of what we said earlier about the christology of the ancient Church it will be seen that this brings us back to the question whether the relation between Jesus and God is to be interpreted metaphysically with the help of the concept of a human and a divine nature and of their unity in the one person of Jesus or whether the unity of Jesus with God must be understood historically. As everyone knows, nothing is said about this in the New Testament, at any rate not directly. The New Testament does not even ask the question. But it does speak of the relation between Jesus and God. Indeed one may properly say that this is the central topic of its message; for when it speaks of God's turning towards us men it does so always by saying that this takes place in and through Jesus. Now it cannot be doubted for a moment that in the New Testament the relation of Jesus to God is understood historically, and not metaphysically in the sense of the dogma of the ancient Church. This is already shown by the fact that it speaks of the unity of Jesus with God by saying that God's turning towards us is an event which takes place in and through Jesus.

But now we must envisage clearly what is in question when we ask about the historical character of this turning of God towards us in and through Jesus. What is meant here is not what is usually thought of when reference is made to the 'redemptive facts' (*Heilstatsachen*). It is not the 'objective' series of occurrences. One may rather say that this question about the historical character (*Geschichtlichkeit*) is directed towards the actual secret of the revelation, the secret which the dogmatists of the ancient Church, making use of the concepts provided by late Greek metaphysics as the only instruments at their disposal, tried to interpret (or more exactly, as one must no doubt say, to describe periphrastically while preserving its character as a secret) in the mystery of the unity of the divine with the human nature in the one person of Christ. They also knew that here and only here, that is to say in the concealment (*Verborgenheit*) of the unity of the Father with the Son, there takes place salvation (*Heil*) in eternity and in time, and for this reason they directed towards it the whole of their thought and the whole of their devotion.[1] For here there arise 'the hills of God, indissoluble, in eternal validity, for us *pro nobis*, but also without us and against us, *sine nobis* and *contra nos*, despite the world's unbelief'. In spite of all their venerable and profound qualities, which no one who understands the matter will contest, the metaphysical concepts of the dogma of the ancient Church have lost their meaning for us, not, it must be repeated once again, because of science and still less because of a 'fashionable philosophy' but as a consequence of the effect of the Christian faith on the general life of the mind;

---

[1] *An-dacht* 'thinking of': a play on the etymology of the word *Andacht* 'devotion, worship, prayer'. TRANSLATOR.

and that is why at this point, with reference to the actual secret of the revelation, namely the unity of the Father with the Son, inquiry must be made into the question of history. Certainly the purpose of raising the question is not to break down the secret. That is no more possible for the historical interpretation and no more its intention than it was for the metaphysics of the old dogma. On the contrary, like the old metaphysics the historical interpretation aims at preserving intact the secret of the redemptive events which since they take place between God and Jesus are at once human and divine. It aims to preserve this secret as the secret it is, but as a historical one.

This expression 'as a historical one' has two implications which nevertheless are in effect one and the same: first that the event takes place in eternity between God and Jesus and second that it takes place in time between Jesus and the world. We are alluding to the secret of the first event, the eternal event, when we speak of it as what takes place between the Father and the Son. The secret of the second, the temporal event is what we mean when we speak of the earthly life and destiny of Jesus. And yet these are not two secrets of different kinds or two events of different kinds. They are the one secret of the turning of God toward us in Jesus Christ. This secret is shown to be what it is precisely by the fact that we never can and never may speak of it otherwise than by reference to the way in which each of these events is implied in the other. In the one, the eternal event between the Father and the Son, what is meant is the world, we men, and it is only to this extent that this event concerns us. In the other, the temporal event between Jesus and the world in the earthly life and destiny of Jesus, what is meant is the eternal unity of the Father and the Son, and it is only in this way that there takes place in this event the unity of Jesus with the world and of the world with

Him. But this oneness is in both cases a historical oneness.

Luther's hymn *Christians Rejoice*[1] tells of this twofold history in words which cannot be bettered. His one reference to it is in the line: 'He said to His dear Son: "The time has come to have mercy" '; and his second is in the line: 'He said to me: "Hold fast to Me." ' And he asserts the unity in the brief phrase: 'The Son obeyed the Father.' As this obedience is the one thing which indissolubly links the eternal and the temporal history, so it marks both the unity of the Father with the Son and the unity of Jesus with the world. But what kind of obedience is this? It is clear from the outset that it is not the same as the obedience which we mean in our everyday use of the word. It is extremely closely connected with what is conveyed by the word responsibility, though this term again is to be taken in the special sense which we have already made clear. The particular quality of this obedience can no doubt be characterized most surely by reference to that 'not of Himself', *ouk aph' heautou*, which is repeated like a refrain throughout the whole of St. John's gospel. The essential nature of the unity of the Son with the Father and of the Father with the Son is defined with extreme exactness by this in conjunction with the other saying which rings out even more frequently, the saying about Jesus's 'being sent' and about the Father's 'having sent' Him. This unity does not only apply to the doing and the speaking of the Son; it permeates and dominates His being. Fatherhood and sonhood are two but are contingent upon one another and in their twofoldness they are one, the one element, filled with the divine *majestas*, in which Jesus lives here on earth, and in which He lives, as He who is sent into the world by the Father, in order to take His own, the world, with Him into it so that they like Him may have life in it. 'And the

[1] *Nun freut euch, liebe Christen g'mein.*

73

glory'—the Greek *doxa*, which we have just translated as *majestas*—'And the glory which thou gavest me I have given them; that they may be one, even as we are one: I in them and thou in me, that they may be made perfect in one; and that the world may know that thou hast sent me, and lovest them, even as thou lovest me' (John 17.22f.).

It is to this obedience that the prologue to St. John's gospel refers when it speaks of the archetypal Word which is at once the Word of creation and the Word of redemption, *ho logos sarx egeneto*, the Word which was in the beginning and which was with God and God was the Word and by it all became and without it nothing became which did become and it became flesh and dwelt among us; this obedience is the redemptive event which takes place in Jesus's delivery of His message of salvation, and it is what is meant by the saying in the synagogue at Nazareth: 'This day is this scripture fulfilled in your ears' (Luke 4.21); and it is consequently this obedience also which takes place in the birth, the life and passion and the death and resurrection of Jesus and which manifests itself in these events. It is because this obedience is rendered in these events that what takes place in this way between the one man Jesus of Nazareth and the world takes place in eternity between the Father and the Son. And it is therefore also through the power of this obedience to unite God and the world that there takes place the event of its being proclaimed and heard. If one enquires after the 'history which has happened' and which happens until the end of the world, then one must enquire after this obedience and after that which takes place in it. Otherwise one is left with only the factual occurrences, the *res gestae*, which cannot in any way be believed in.

It is this *kerygma* and no other which is referred to in that assertion which has given so much offence, the assertion that the crucified and risen One comes before us in His Word and nowhere else.[1] On the basis of what has already been stated we may say without hesitation that this assertion does not at all mean that the person of Jesus and His history have been replaced by a *kerygma* which is entirely devoid of history and which is moreover only a more or less arbitrary product of the earliest Christian Church, 'a free interpretation of processes of consciousness'. What it does mean is to point out with all possible emphasis that the person and the history of Jesus are present in this *kerygma*, present with the same historical presence as that with which He is present on each separate occasion both with the disciples and with the Church of our own day and the Church of the future.

But to this it will be replied that the actual cause of the offence given by this assertion lies in its being linked with the further assertion that what the New Testament says about the person and history of Jesus is at least in part mythological and that these mythical elements ought to be eliminated. Here it is necessary to draw a distinction between the mythological manner of the New Testament statements, which is what is meant by 'mythical elements', and the statements themselves, i.e. *what* they state or intend to state. The historical approach to the New Testament, which in view of its method is referred to as the 'existential interpretation', would see no meaning in itself if while eliminating the mythological manner of the New Testament statements it were also to try to eliminate the matter of these statements. For indeed what is conveyed in these statements is precisely the history of Jesus, though certainly it is history in the sense of the New Testament *kerygma*. And if one speaks of a 'critical' interpretation of the

[1] Bultmann, *Kerygma und Mythos*, I, p. 50. (Cf. *Kerygma and Myth*, S.P.C.K., 1953, p. 41.)

mythology of the New Testament this does not mean at all that this interpretation borrows its criteria from some modern *Weltanschauung* as of course a certain species of theologians, whose dread of science can never be allayed immediately, suppose when they hear the word 'critical'. This interpretation takes its criteria from the understanding of history which is inherent in the New Testament and which is expressed in it clearly enough in spite of the mythical elements of its language. And guided by this criterion the 'critical interpretation' endeavours to show what the New Testament is trying to say in that element of mythology which it contains.

It is only if what the New Testament mythology states with regard to the history of Jesus is clearly understood in this way on the basis of the historical character of the New Testament *kerygma*, as we have already described it, that it will become entirely clear that to speak of 'objective factualness' is to be guilty of a miserable rationalization of the New Testament history, which is not very surprising if one takes into account the sources of this view in the history of philosophy. All that is surprising is that this view should claim to conform to the New Testament and to its historical character. Precisely this rationalization must at all costs be avoided, and if the choice were still open to us we should be obliged to say we prefer the mythology of the New Testament to the 'objective historicity (*Historizität*)' of the so-called redemptive facts (*Heilstatsachen*), for by this rationalization the New Testament message loses its own historical character.

From this standpoint it is now possible also to understand what is meant when it is said of the *kerygma* that 'it is essential to its tradition'—which one must here interpret as meaning both what it conveys and the manner in which it conveys it —'that the historical trustworthiness of its contents must not be called in question.[1] This implies that to call it in question in this way, if this is done in good faith and conveys any sort of meaning at all, is and must be to try to grasp the contents of the tradition by reference to the intramundane context, by 're-producing facts from the past in their pure mundane matter-of-factness',[2] as is indeed the proper business of the historical investigator. But the history which the *kerygma* transmits, and which takes place in actual presence in the *kerygma* through being transmitted in it, has precisely the peculiarity that it does not arise from the intramundane context, and by the same token its past is not one to which one can look back as one looks back to what has at some time occurred within the intramundane context and is now past. It arises from that self-same obedience from which the *kerygma* arises, and this obedience in turn is the response to what Luther in the hymn which we have already quoted expresses in the words: 'He turns his fatherly heart towards me.' This mercifulness is 'new every morning', and that is why one must no doubt say that this history is eschatological.

It is certainly the case that such a redemptive event as the Cross of Christ has its origin in time in the historical occurrence of the crucifixion of Jesus of Nazareth; but one would be setting one's reliance upon the world and upon the intra-mundane context of events within it if one were to seek in this for the trustworthiness of the contents of the tradition. The tradition must carry within itself and nowhere else the trust-worthiness which is here being enquired for. For indeed faith in the *kerygma*, if it is real belief in it, can be nothing other than faith in God, faith in the truth of the saying that 'He turned His fatherly heart towards me'. This turning of God towards us

[1] Cf. Bultmann, *Kerygma und Mythos*, I, p. 147.
[2] Cf. Bultmann, *Kerygma und Mythos*, I, p. 146.

takes place in the *kerygma* wherever and whenever it is proclaimed and heard, and it is of this and of nothing else that Bultmann is speaking in the following sentences: 'What Jesus is for me is not limited to—and indeed is not at all perceptible in—the appearance which He presents when He is viewed from the standpoint of historical investigation. He is not to be questioned with regard to His historical origin, and indeed His real significance (*Bedeutung*) is to be seen only when no such question is raised. His history and His Cross are not to be questioned with regard to their historical basis; for the significance (*Bedeutung*) of His history arises from what God wishes to say to me through it. And thus His personality is not to be grasped in its full significance (*Bedeutsamkeit*) by reference to the intramundane context; that is to say, in mythological language, He comes from eternity and His origin is not a human or natural one.'[1] Clearly the sense in which Bultmann employs the concept of significance (*Bedeutung* or *Bedeutsamkeit*) must be understood by reference to his whole argument, for since this concept occupies a central position there, as is clear indeed from the few sentences we have just quoted, there is good reason to suppose that the term is not to be taken in its everyday connotation without further definition. And a small effort of memory will be sufficient to recall that the verb *bedeuten* is occasionally used in a sense which differs from the everyday one. This is in the sense in which one says '*er bedeutete mich*',[2] which means more than 'he said to me' and more or less the

[1] Bultmann in *Kerygma und Mythos*, I, p. 45.

[2] This construction usually implies a correction or a command. Here it seems to correspond to the seventeenth-century use of 'signify' for 'notify' or 'inform'. Perhaps the ambiguity is best rendered in English by retaining the verb 'signify' and reading into it and its derivatives both its usual sense of 'mean' or 'betoken' and the sense in which it is used in such expressions as 'he signified his intention to me'. TRANSLATOR.

same as 'he made a momentous declaration to me'. This would explain how Bultmann can say that 'the significance (*Bedeutung*) of His history is the product of what God wishes to say to me through it'. And such a reading immediately makes clear what Bultmann means when he speaks of the redemptive event as constituting the 'significance' (*Bedeutsamkeit*) of the history of Jesus. In and with this history there takes place the event by which God, in and with this history, signifies something to me (i.e. notifies me of something), namely the fact and the manner of Christ's being the salvation of man and of the world. Certainly Bultmann's language here is very 'down to earth' if one compares it with the language which is generally thought to be appropriate to this theme. Yet there are good reasons which make it at least not altogether out of place to tell the Gospel story in language which does not set out to sound 'edifying'. One very good reason is that in this way one is compelled to think very exactly about what one is saying and is prevented from abandoning oneself to that remarkable but neither intellectually nor spiritually defensible attitude in which one preaches for preaching's sake. But no matter whether his style be 'down to earth' or 'edifying', what is of decisive importance for the theologian, that is to say for his ability to fulfil his mission, is that he should be able to give a clear and so far as possible an unequivocal account of what he has to say.

In my opinion this aim has been achieved in these sentences of Bultmann's. Admittedly this seems to be contradicted by the circumstance that a very large number of theologians have failed to understand them and that in some cases as we shall later have to show they have misunderstood them in a manner which indicates an extreme lack of insight and deliberation. On the basis of what we have already made clear it is not very difficult to see the reason for this incomprehension. The expression 'significance' as Bultmann employs it is very closely linked with the interpretation of history which it is the purpose of the existential philosophy to develop and elucidate. And, as we have seen, this interpretation is directly opposed to the subject-object pattern of thought which has exercised its influence upon modern historical thought, among other things, and consequently also upon theology in so far as it is concerned with history.[1] Its purpose is therefore to set history free from the objectivity which pervades it and in which it is deadened as soon as it is in one way or another thought of as an object. This emancipation can be accomplished only by understanding history and the character of history (*Geschichtlichkeit*) in their own historical essential nature, or, as we may rather say since this word is more readily grasped in its verbal[2] significance, in their own force (*Walten*). This is true of history and of the character of history in general, no matter what may take place within it, and it is no less true of that history which is the concern of theology.

If this means that we must say of history in general that (to use Heidegger's terms) an event 'un-conceals' (*ent-birgt*) itself in it and that this event which un-conceals itself is to be perceived only by means of a corresponding 'self-unconcealment' on the part of him for whom or to whom it happens,

---

[1] Incidentally, if one believes oneself obliged to approach the redemptive history and its reality from the point of view of this epistemology which is governed by the subject-object pattern of thought, what right has one to accuse of '*weltanschaulich* bias' and so forth, someone who thinks that it may at any rate be possible to derive from another philosophy a tenable interpretation of the essential nature of history?

[2] *Walten* is unmistakably an infinitive used substantivally. *Wesen*, here translated 'essential nature', is in lay parlance a noun, 'essence' or 'being', so that there is a danger that one may overlook the fact that it is also the infinitive of Heidegger's verb *wesen*. TRANSLATOR.

then it follows that the same is no less true of the history which we call the revelational history of God because in it God unconceals Himself for us. This self-unconcealment (*Sichentbergen*) of God, through which alone the New Testament history is redemptive history, is what is intended to be denoted by that expression 'significance' which in the 'demythologization' controversy has given rise to so much misguided indignation. The term is unequivocal and clear for anyone who approaches this theology seriously and open-mindedly, and indeed in the sentences which we have just quoted Bultmann interprets it himself as meaning 'what God wants to say to me through the history of Jesus'. But of course it must inevitably remain totally incomprehensible for anyone who simply does not see that he must clearly envisage what he is saying when he speaks of history as an object because he has come to take for granted the philosophy of the subject-object scheme of thought, whereby, what is more, it has ceased to be philosophy but has not for that reason become theology. Nor indeed will he understand that his conception of the history of God as 'objective factualness' is what is described in the sentence in which Heidegger characterizes the 'conception (*das Vorstellen*) since Descartes': 'It is not that which is present which exercises its force, but it is the attack or seizure which predominates.'[1] That is to say, the attack or seizure in which man makes himself master of history, since in this 'conception' he is 'himself the measure of all the yardsticks with which there is gauged and apportioned or computed whatever can be regarded as certain, that is to say true, and that is to say being (*seiend*').[2]

[1] *Nicht das Anwesende waltet, sondern der Angriff herrscht.*
[2] Heidegger, *Holzwege*, pp. 101f.

IX

Conclusion

KINDER is quite right when he says that theology will not become free from a scientific concept which is alien to it until it takes seriously as a reality that reality which discloses itself in faith.[1] But the point is that it must take seriously precisely this reality and not some other reality which is suggested to it by an alien and irrelevant scientific concept. Christian faith is faith in the Word of God, whatever one may say about its 'objects' if one assumes that it implies belief in something other than this. It is faith in God's promise (*Verspruch*), and consequently the reality with which it is concerned is never any other reality than that of the Word. In any case it is certainly not what one refers to as an 'objective' or 'factual' reality. For after all what is meant by Luther's reforming rediscovery of the gospel is that everything that is in any way connected with the revelation derives its revelational character from this word. That is what accounts for his insistence on the 'by faith alone', the *sola fide*, and that is what is at the root of his doctrine of justification. We have already made frequent reference to the subject-object pattern of thought and to the nefarious rôle which it has played in theology: if the shortcomings of this way of thinking can ever be made clear, it might well be supposed that this would be the case when one hears and says that God reveals Himself in the Word. And indeed for the

[1] *Ein Wort lutherischer Theologie,* p. 51.

82

Christian faith He does not merely do this incidentally, but both in the Old and in the New Testament wherever there is emphatic reference to God's revelation there is reference also to His Word. In support of this statement it will suffice to point to the fact that the two parts of the Bible are called the Old and the New Testament, or to the fact that Luther is of the opinion that he can and must designate the revelation of God in its entire contents with the concepts of law and gospel. It is not difficult to see that this placing of the Word in the central position as regards the revelation does not in any way exclude the deed of God, but we must look more closely if we are to recognize that the relation of the Word and the deed in the revelation is not such that the deed comes first and is followed as a kind of directive or commentary by the Word. Nor, of course, is the opposite the case: first the Word and then the deed. On the contrary, what is peculiar to the way in which the divine revelation comes to us is that the deed takes place through the Word and in the Word. And this means that the deed can be understood as the deed of God only if it is grasped in the Word, that is to say in the hearing of the Word, grasped or more exactly and correctly 'suffered' (*erlitten*), for in addition to its usual connotations *leiden* (suffer) also bears the sense which we attach to it in the idiom *ich mag dich leiden*.[1] The deed and the deeds of God have therefore a verbal (*worthaft* or *wortlich*) character. Briefly then we may say that God's Word is an address to a listener, but certainly it is an address only in a very restricted sense, and this sense may perhaps most easily be defined by once more employing the word 'promise' (*Verspruch*) in the sense of engagement or betrothal (*Verlöbnis*), for this term is used in the Old Testament, especially by Hosea (2.21), in speaking of the covenant of

---

[1] 'I can suffer you', meiotic for 'I like you'. TRANSLATOR.

Yahweh with Israel. What takes place in the Word which is this divine engagement (*Verspruch*) is consequently no more and no less than that God promises (*verspricht*) Himself to man as his God. (This is very much what Luther means when he says that God promises (*zusagt*) Himself to him.) And this in turn means that God, in promising Himself to man, does not only give him life, making him be 'of God in the sight of God' (2 Cor. 2.17), in the sense in which St. Paul says of God that 'He calls that which is not, as that which is' (Rom. 4.17).[1] But He also at the same time calls this man whom He has called into being, telling him that as this man who has been called into being he may exist (*da sei*—may be there) for Him. I would like to point out in passing that there is a very great deal to be learnt from Luther on this subject. But also from Heidegger. And for this reason Bultmann is probably only too right when he expresses the opinion that the theologians might very well feel horrified at the fact that philosophy today knows very many things which they, the theologians, ought actually to know too, but which are for the most part outside their ken.

If the Word in and through which God reveals Himself is of this nature, that is to say if it is a Word in the proper sense of the term and not merely, as we no doubt generally understand it, an imparting of information or a notification about it, then it is of course immediately evident that this Word can have

---

[1] Gogarten here uses Luther's version: '*Er ruft dem, das nicht ist, dass es sei*'— 'He calls to that which is not, that it may be (or is).' Luther's use of the dative *dem* excludes the possibility of reading 'call' in the sense of 'summon'. In the following sentence and elsewhere Gogarten constructs *rufen* with the accusative of the person called, so that either meaning (or both) may be intended. Luther's dependent clause may be read as statement or command or purpose or result, but it does not correspond to the English 'as though it were'. The dependent clause in Gogarten's next sentence has the same construction. TRANSLATOR.

nothing whatever to do with the reality which one can grasp by means of that subject-object pattern of thought of which we have been speaking. If one nevertheless attempts to grasp it in this way, one will fail hopelessly. Those who seek for an 'objective revelational reality' do not at all realize to what an extent they are held fast in the ' "Babylonian captivity" imposed on them by a scientific concept which is essentially alien' to theology. Certainly they want to escape from this captivity, but with every thought that leads them in this direction they find themselves fettered all the more securely.

Bultmann's theology may appear to his opponents to be in direct conflict with what they call the 'authentic tradition', but, however repugnant this may be to them, one cannot do otherwise than advise them with the greatest possible urgency to desist from depriving themselves, by their false or inadequate understanding of this theology, of the assistance which it alone can render them in thinking about—and in learning to speak about—the reality of the revelation in such a manner that it is understood in the sense which is in accordance with the New Testament and with the principles of the Reformation, that is to say as the verbal (*worthaft*) reality, as the one reality which is the reality of the Word of God, and as nothing else. For it is to this goal that Bultmann's 'existential interpretation' is intended to lead; and this is the purpose which underlies what he has to say about 'significance' (*Bedeutsamkeit*). It is scarcely necessary to say explicitly that this advice is not intended to mean that they must adhere to the procedures which Bultmann employs or that they must accept the detailed conclusions of his studies. Bultmann himself is well aware that the work which remains to be done in this field is so great and so far-reaching that it 'cannot devolve upon any one individual but demands the full time and energy of an entire generation of theologians'.[1] But what we do mean when we offer this advice to Bultmann's opponents is that they should allow him to direct their attention to the problem of the *genus* of the revelational reality, for in studying his work the question of the *genus* of the divine Word becomes a more urgent one than it is in the general run of theology where the Word of God seems to be taken quite as a matter of course. This Word is in truth a Word *sui generis*. And, as I have already said, we can learn what this *genus* is from Luther better than from anyone else. It is really, in the proper sense of the term, a Word. And the revelational reality is of the same *genus*.

To indicate what this means it may be sufficient to refer by way of example to one problem which figures prominently in the controversy about demythologization. This is the problem of the New Testament miracles. Kinder warns theologians against 'bowing to the claim to unconditional validity which is asserted on behalf of the reality criteria of the natural man'.[2] This warning may be taken to mean that theology is not to allow its attitude to these miracles to be dictated to it by a 'scientific concept of reality which has its roots in the natural man's feeling for life',[3] a concept which would require it either to deny the miracles, or, which adds up to the same thing, to interpret them out of existence by rationalizing or allegorizing them. But now, if we assume that the reality with which theology is concerned is the verbal (*worthaft*) reality of the Word of God and no other, this warning must bear the further implication that theology should also beware of allowing its attitude to the miracles of the New Testament to be dictated to it by the reality criteria of that 'natural man'

[1] *Kerygma und Mythos*, I, p. 27.
[2] *Ein Wort lutherischer Theologie*, p. 52.
[3] *Ein Wort lutherischer Theologie*, p. 51.

whose reality includes miracles entirely as a matter of course. Kinder knows as well as I do that miracles as such are not by any means a specifically New Testament phenomenon. It is therefore quite possible that theology is 'bowing to the reality criteria of the natural man' just as much in accepting the miracles as in rejecting them. What theology must do, if it is to be Christian theology, is to seek after the verbal (*worthaft*) reality and to enquire whether this reality reveals itself in the miracle. Bultmann is saying the same thing when he speaks of the 'significance' (*Bedeutsamkeit*) which is to be enquired after. This applies not only to the New Testament miracles but also and in a still more urgent sense to the redemptive history (*Heilsgeschehen*), in the specific meaning of the term, to which both the Old and the New Testament, each in its special way, bear witness. But if instead of this one does what the authors of *Ein Wort lutherischer Theologie* are doing, and sets out to find some 'objectivity' or 'factualness' in the revelational history, then indeed, whatever line one may take, one is 'bowing to the reality criteria of the natural man'. To objectify God and His Word is to deny Him. It is horrifying to see how in our time, when this has really ceased to be in the least necessary, almost the whole of theological thought, with few and indeed ever fewer exceptions, is moving in this disastrous direction.

This situation is a very grave one and must have extremely far-reaching consequences for the future of the Protestant Church. For it means that the Church has less and less access to that from which alone she draws her life and that which it is her duty to impart to the man of today, namely the Word of God. And it also means, to express it briefly and perhaps a little too bluntly, that despite all the earnestness and the diligence of the Church's theologians and clergy in their many-sided labours which in the general difficult spiritual and material circumstances of our time are becoming ever more comprehensive and which threaten to exhaust their forces, despite these efforts which no one who knows of them will contest them, they do not understand what is taking place today in the world of thought. What is taking place is, to quote Heidegger again, the merging 'of the modern essence, as it achieves completion, in the matter-of-course. Only when this has been philosophically assured will the scene be set for an original calling in question of being, a calling in question which provides room for the decision as to whether being shall once again become capable of a god and whether the essence of the truth of being involves the essence of man more incipiently in its claim. It is only at the point where the completion of the modern age attains to the relentlessness of its proper greatness that future history is prepared.'[1] In its application to theology this means that in the study of the New Testament and also of the history of dogma the principles of historical and literary criticism are to be applied 'honestly and vigorously', which, if it is intended seriously, can only mean unreservedly and with the 'relentlessness of its proper greatness'. In this way theology is to break free at last from its enslavement to the metaphysical categories of late Greek philosophy, an enslavement which it has inherited from the dogmatic elaborations of the ancient Church and which still paralyses the thinking of those who

---

[1] *Holzwege*, p. 103. English can hardly do justice to the rich metaphorical texture of Heidegger's language. In German the passage reads as follows: *Es ereignet sich . . . die Einschmelzung des sich vollendenden neuzeitlichen Wesens in das Selbstverständliche. Erst wenn dieses weltanschaulich gesichert ist, wächst der mögliche Nährboden für eine ursprüngliche Fragwürdigkeit des Seins, die den Spielraum der Entscheidung darüber öffnet, ob das Sein noch einmal eines Gottes fähig wird, ob das Wesen der Wahrheit des Seins das Wesen des Menschen anfänglicher in den Anspruch nimmt. Dort, wo die Vollendung der Neuzeit die Rücksichtslosigkeit der ihr eigenen Grösse erlangt, wird allein die zukünftige Geschichte vorbereitet.'* TRANSLATOR.

accept it and prevents them from following the straight and open road that leads to modern historical living and also to Luther who for his part, with his doctrine of the Word and of faith, was in the one crucial respect the first to break the spell. When this is achieved such chimeras and phantasmagorias as 'objective factualness' and 'objectively real events' will quite automatically disappear.

For indeed these are nothing but the indescribably wretched and meagre remnants which are all that a rationalistic and scientifically and technologically minded generation preserved of the metaphysical categories of the theology of the ancient Church, categories which in their day still retained the profundity and the truly philosophical significance of Greek thought. To set theology free from these is the service which is rendered to it by a resolute historical study which need be afraid of no conclusions that it may reach so long as it remains critical, that is to say scientific, and that again is to say so long as it does not depart from the purpose which is implicit in its method and deviate into *Weltanschauung*. It is only if this historical study is unreservedly acknowledged that there can be an understanding of history which recognizes its essential nature. It is typical of Künneth's own philosophical position, the position of one who is held captive by a *Weltanschauung*, when he says of Bultmann, probably by way of making an excuse for him, that he 'suffers from the difficulty of the historical investigator'. I think I may say the opposite. There can be no question of Bultmann's 'suffering' in the sense in which the term is intended here. For, in whatever form it comes, the truth shall make us free. Of course one must have the courage to be free, and this courage can come only when one knows upon what this freedom is founded. Now the freedom of man is founded upon the freedom of God, and this freedom comes to us in God's Word. The road to this freedom is precisely the road which is opened up by critical historical study and by reflection on history, in the sense, of course, in which it must be pursued in theology. It is here that theology fulfils part of its appointed task in contributing to 'the setting of the scene for an original calling in question of being which provides room for the decision as to whether being is once again to become capable of a god and whether the essence of the truth of being involves man more incipiently in its claim'. For this, however, it is necessary that all its questioning and thinking should be directed to the reality and to the *genus* of the Word of God. This alone is and must be the purpose of the controversy concerning demythologization.

Index of Subjects

Analogia entis, 64

Confession of sin, 53
Corpus Christi mysticum, 36

Existential interpretation, 48, 53-62, 65-8, 75, 80, 85
Existentialism, 56, 62
Existential philosophy, 61-5
Existentiell, 56-8, 62

Fides historica, 13

Glory, 73-4
Greek philosophy, 21-2, 64, 71, 88-9
Guilt, 49, 60

Historical method, 18-20, 25, 30-1
Historicism, 57
Historicity, 19, 76

Kerygma, 37, 55, 66, 68-9, 74-7

Medieval philosophy, 21-5

Metaphysics, 13, 16, 21, 23-6, 31-8, 43-7, 60, 70-2, 88
Miracles, 40, 86-7
Myth, 66-7, 75-6

Promissio dei, 14, 16, 82-4

Rationalism, 59, 76, 89
Responsibility, 19-20, 23, 26-33, 49-54, 60-2, 73
Roman Catholicism, 13, 24
Romanticism, 27

Sacramentalism, 24, 36, 44-5
Significance, 78-81, 85, 87
Sin, 20, 29, 49, 52-4, 60
Subject and object, 50-2, 55-60, 62-7, 80-2, 85
Supernatural and suprahistorical, 47-8

Verbal inspiration, 12

Weltanschauung, 13, 16, 18, 25-6, 58-9, 61-2, 76, 80, 89
World, 52-3

Index of Names